Robert Graves
The Centenary Selected Poems

Robert Graves Programme
General Editor: Patrick J.M. Quinn

The Centenary Selected Poems
edited by Patrick J.M. Quinn

Collected Writings on Poetry
edited by Paul O'Prey

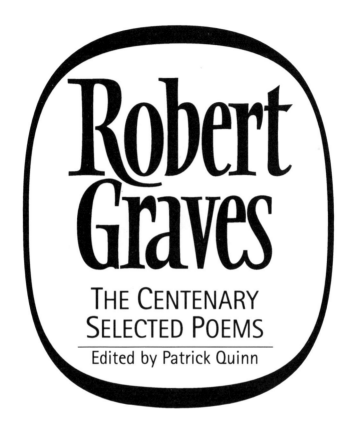

Robert Graves

THE CENTENARY
SELECTED POEMS

Edited by Patrick Quinn

CARCANET

First published in Great Britain in 1995 by
Carcanet Press Limited
402-406 Corn Exchange Buildings
Manchester M4 3BY

A CIP catalogue record for this book
is available from the British Library.
ISBN 1 85754 126 X

The publisher acknowledges financial
assistance from the Arts Council of England

Set in 10pt Meridien by Bryan Williamson, Frome
Printed and bound in England by SRP Ltd, Exeter

Funded by
THE
ARTS
COUNCIL
OF ENGLAND

Contents

Introduction

It is perhaps because the poetry of Robert Graves defies categorization that many critics have been tempted to overlook or underestimate his contribution to English literature in their studies of English poetic movements in the twentieth century. Often, Graves is given a token nod as a mythographer like Yeats, as a Georgian like de la Mare, or even as a romantic poet like Dylan Thomas (whose poetry Graves loathed). Generally speaking, however, Graves's wide-ranging poetic achievements have not been granted the critical recognition and secure standing that they deserve.

One factor which may have contributed to this less than enthusiastic critical reception could be Graves's apparent unwillingness to fit into English poetic 'culture'. Graves committed the same major sin as two other undervalued English writers of this century, Richard Aldington and Lawrence Durrell, who chose to bid goodbye to the strictures of English society and to write their most successful works abroad. English literary critics generally have a difficult time forgiving writers who thrive in foreign climes and who eschew the London literary establishment. It is not altogether surprising, therefore, that Graves's literary reputation is much more firmly established in North America (as are the reputations of Aldington and Durrell) than in England, whilst his compatriots tend to remember him primarily for his authorship of *I Claudius* (a novel which Graves himself admitted was merely a pot-boiler), so successfully adapted for television.

In fact, it is highly likely that Graves would not have minded being ignored by the literary critics of today. He speaks like a man with nothing to lose when he refers to his audience in 'The Reader Over My Shoulder' (which is unfortunately placed on page 58 of the most recent edition of *Collected Poems*, when it ought to stand instead at the beginning of the volume). Here, Graves points to his critics with more than a touch of cynicism when he states,

> You, reading over my shoulder, peering beneath
> My writing arm – I suddenly feel your breath
>   Hot on my hand or on my nape,
> So interrupt my theme, scratching these few
> Words on the margin for you, namely you,
>   Too-human shape fixed in that shape: ...
>
> For you in strutting, you in sycophancy
> Have played too long this other self of me,
>   Doubling the part of judge and patron

With that of creaking grind-stone to my wit.
Know me, have done: I am a proud spirit
And you forever clay. Have done!

Nevertheless, the majority of critics who have reviewed or criticized Graves's work in any depth have been impressed by his craftsmanship and poetic innovation. Very few critics would counter the argument that Graves's love lyrics are amongst the finest written in a poetic era noticeably lacking in poetry celebrating love. Nor could any earnest reader of Graves's poetry fail to appreciate his wry cynicism and caustic humour, his enjoyment of the unlikely predicaments in which lovers land themselves. Graves is a truly Protean poet, and his ability to re-incarnate himself in a variety of ways as a poetic commentator of his time appears to be as effective as that of the goddess Astarte herself.

The most recently published major collection of Graves's poetry was assembled in 1975, and twenty years later it is still valuable in that it incorporates the nucleus of Graves's poetic reputation. The poems included in that collection are the end-products of Graves's obsession with revision, and have been polished as smoothly as poems can be. Many critics adhere to Randall Jarrell's view, expressed in the *Yale Review* in 1956, that nearly every change which Graves made to his originals tightened or sharpened a poetic image or metaphor. I am not so sure that I agree. Poetic tastes apart, Graves's revisions – which admittedly often have the effect of improving technically a line or an image – sometimes delicately alter the tone of the poem in an essential way. Graves's revisions of 'The Pier-Glass', for example, change the integral meaning of the original poem.

One reason for this new selection of his poems, therefore, is to allow Graves's original voice to be heard in its historical context: the nightmarish effects of Graves's neurasthenia on his war poetry, for example, are clearly manifest and are not tempered or toned down in any way by the later influence of the White Goddess; similarly, Graves's juvenile fantasies such as 'In the Wilderness' are left intact and unaffected by Graves's subsequent maturity. The progression from psychological poetry of the 1920s, written when Graves was trying to expunge the war neuroses from his mind (and much of which he later suppressed for what seem today to be capricious reasons), through to his Muse-driven verse of the 1960s offers the modern reader an opportunity to follow Graves's poetic development from aspiring schoolboy poet to mature philosopher, who was ultimately to find poetic fulfilment under the benevolent protection of the Black Goddess.

In this selection, Graves's work has been divided into five categories, each of which marks a clear delineation between one phase and the next of his poetic career. The first section typifies Graves's Georgian phase (1914-1921), during which the then naïve poet was under the tutelage of Edward Marsh and attempted, not very successfully, to confront the decidedly 'un-Georgian' subject-matter of the Great War. Graves's ineffective attempt to escape from the nightmares of the trenches into the comfortable world of nursery rhyme and ballad rounds off this section. The second phase of Graves's poetic development may be classified as the Modernist Delvings (1921-1926). During this period Graves attempted, through experimentation with psychology, logic and relativistic philosophy, to find a means of healing his damaged self, to find some sense of order and harmony in a world which for him was still haunted by images of war. It was not until Laura Riding entered on the scene in 1927, and was able to provide Graves with a sense of certainty, that his poetry began to renounce the purely sensual aspects of life and to move beyond the physical and emotional to an awareness of that which was outside human nature – an awareness of timelessness. The following sixteen years of Riding's disciplined regime (1927-1942) was a period in which Graves's poetry became markedly more cerebral and introspective and often seems to be clever for cleverness's sake. The poems are often aggressive and combative, but Graves's faith in Riding did more than enable him to develop a new poetic voice: it also led him out of the endless vortex of a post-war world bereft – as he saw it – of purpose and discipline.

In 1942, three years after Riding's defection with the farmer/philosopher Schuyler Jackson, Graves wrote a poem called 'Mid-Winter Awakening', which in effect announced his liberation from Riding's influence and celebrated the recovery of his poetic powers. The poem was ostensibly written in dedication to Graves's second wife, Beryl, but its theme looks forward to the poet's adoration for his inspiration, his White Goddess. The so-called 'White Goddess period' runs from 1943 to 1959, during which time a vast amount of Graves's poetry was concerned with fealty to a cruel and demanding Muse whose role was to command absolute servitude in exchange for frustration and suffering, causing the poet to write more proficiently about the nature of love. (In these poems love might better be defined as a combination of lust and fear than as affection in its traditional sense.) This thematic superstructure was imposed on nearly all of Graves's important poems of the period. Even those poems which are not specifically concerned with this theme are linked in some way to it. (A number of Graves's poems of this period, for example, attack males who have rejected the view that the female sex is naturally superior.)

Graves's rather masochistic vision of life underwent a transformation in the early 1960s, which ushered in for Graves the period of the Black Goddess. During this last phase of his career, Graves enjoyed a more positive and satisfying relationship with his Muse-figure. In the final poems of his life, Graves celebrated the intellectual pleasure and emotional joy which he derived from his 'musings', but his poetry of the last period also manifests a stoical awareness that love must run its cyclical course and that every poet must be prepared for the inevitable loss of his muse.

A NOTE ON THE TEXT

The poems are arranged in chronological order. Where a poem first appeared in a magazine, I have used that text where possible. I have taken the liberty of silently correcting obvious misprints and misspellings. Graves re-titled many of his early poems; the later titles are included in parentheses.

Any editor of a selection is aware of the impossibility of pleasing all readers, and this is especially so where Graves is concerned, since he compiled his own *Selected Poems* for Penguin. How can one compete with the author's choice? The answer is simply that one cannot. But the editor of a new selection can throw a different light on well-known poems by setting them in a particular context, and can bring into the light less-read poems which merit attention. The criteria for this choice were largely historical and developmental. The 150 poems included here seem to me to provide the most satisfying examples of Graves's varying philosophies and experimental techniques, his considerations of love and war, and his struggles with society. The last phase of his work is least well-represented, partly because it is more easily available, and partly because the poems written under the sway of the Black Goddess are less novel and various than those of the White Goddess phase.

The reproduction of the poems in their original forms and order of publication is intended to allow the reader insight into the ebb and flow of Graves's poetic genius. Ultimately, it is hoped that this new edition will reawaken general readers and academics alike to the extent of the poetic accomplishment of Graves, who was at his peak when Eliot and Auden were in the ascendant, and whose reputation should not be obscured by theirs.

The Georgian Period (1914-1920)

During this period, Graves's earliest works took their impetus from the Georgian tradition, with its emphasis on the beauties of rural life and nature and the musicality of language. Graves's poetic model during this time was Walter de la Mare. A less acknowledged element of Georgian poetry, however, and one which Graves embraced wholeheartedly, was its encouragement of individualism and celebration of sensuality, which had been repressed by the generation preceding Graves and for which the modern world, with its stress on technological advancement over humanitarian concerns, did not bode well. The struggle between individualism/ liberation of the spirit and conformism/repression was exacerbated for Graves during his active service as an officer in the Great War at the age of only nineteen. His poetry of the war period is undeniably accomplished in its ability to depict the horror of incidents such as his experience of Mametz Wood, but it never quite cuts to the quick of the experience itself.

Most critics have decried Graves's attempts to escape his memories of the war by returning to the familiar Georgian mode as being too simplistic. True, Graves did experiment in the immediate post-war period with nursery rhymes, ballads and optimistic love lyrics which, superficially at least, seem rather lightweight. In the later poems of this period, though, Graves speculated on the complexities of love and on the perplexities of existence in poems such as 'Rocky Acres' and 'Lost Love'. By 1920, the intellectual probing and philosophical inquiry which had been prompted to a certain extent by his experiences of war and by his first taste of marriage were already manifesting themselves in Graves's verse and were to become the focus of his agonized self-inquiry in subsequent volumes.

MAJOR POETRY VOLUMES:

Over the Brazier	London: The Poetry Bookshop, 1916
Goliath and David	London: Chiswick Press, 1916
Fairies and Fusiliers	London: William Heinemann, 1917
Treasure Box	London: Chiswick Press, 1919
Country Sentiment	London: Martin Secker, 1920

The Poet in the Nursery

The youngest poet down the shelves was fumbling
    In a dim library, just behind the chair
From which the ancient poet was mum-mumbling
    A song about some Lovers at a Fair,
Pulling his long white beard and gently grumbling
    That rhymes were beastly things and never there.

And as I groped, the whole time I was thinking
    About the tragic poem I'd been writing –
An old man's life of beer and whiskey drinking,
    His years of kidnapping and wicked fighting;
And how at last, into a fever sinking,
    Remorsefully he died, his bedclothes biting.

But suddenly I saw the bright green cover
   Of a thin pretty book right down below;
I snatched it up and turned the pages over,
   To find it full of poetry, and so
Put it down my neck with quick hands like a lover
   And turned to watch if the old man saw it go.

The book was full of funny muddling mazes
   Each rounded off into a lovely song,
And most extraordinary and monstrous phrases
   Knotted with rhymes like a slave-driver's thong,
And metre twisting like a chain of daisies
   With great big splendid words a sentence long.

I took the book to bed with me and gloated,
   Learning the lines that seemed to sound most grand,
So soon the pretty emerald green was coated
   With jam and greasy marks from my hot hand,
While round the nursery for long months there floated
   Wonderful words no one could understand.

Over the Brazier 1916

In the Wilderness

Christ of his gentleness
Thirsting and hungering
Walked in the wilderness;
Soft words of grace He spoke
Unto lost desert-folk
That listened wondering.
He heard the bitterns call
From ruined palace-wall,
Answered them brotherly.
He held communion
With the she-pelican
Of lonely piety.
Basilisk, cockatrice,
Flocked to His homilies,
With mail of dread device,
With monstrous barbéd stings,

With eager dragon-eyes;
Great rats on leather wings
And poor blind broken things,
Foul in their miseries.
And ever with Him went,
Of all His wanderings
Comrade, with ragged coat,
Gaunt ribs – poor innocent –
Bleeding foot, burning throat,
The guileless old scape-goat;
For forty nights and days
Followed in Jesus' ways,
Sure guard behind Him kept,
Tears like a lover wept.

Over the Brazier 1916

Escape

(*August 6th, 1916, Officer previously reported died of wounds now reported wounded, Graves, Capt. R., Royal Welch Fus.*)

...But I *was* dead, an hour or more:
I woke when I'd already passed the door
That Cerberus guards and half-way down the road
To Lethe, as an old Greek sign-post showed.
Above me, on my stretcher swinging by,
I saw new stars in the sub-terrene sky,
A Cross, a Rose in Bloom, a Cage with Bars,
And a barbed Arrow feathered with fine stars.
I felt the vapours of forgetfulness
Float in my nostrils: Oh, may Heaven bless
Dear Lady Proserpine, who saw me wake
And stooping over me, for Henna's sake
Cleared my poor buzzing head and sent me back
Breathless, with leaping heart along the track.
After me roared and clattered angry hosts
Of demons, heroes, and policemen-ghosts.
'Life, life! I can't be dead, I won't be dead:
Damned if I'll die for anyone,' I said...
Cerberus stands and grins above me now,

Wearing three heads, lion and lynx and sow.
'Quick, a revolver! but my Webley's gone,
Stolen...no bombs...no knife...(the crowd swarms on,
Bellows, hurls stones)...not even a honeyed sop...
Nothing...Good Cerberus...Good dog...but stop!
Stay!...a great luminous thought...I do believe
There's still some morphia that I bought on leave.'
Then swiftly Cerberus' wide mouths I cram
With Army biscuit smeared with Tickler's jam;
And Sleep lurks in the luscious plum and apple.
He crunches, swallows, stiffens, seems to grapple
With the all-powerful poppy...then a snore,
A crash; the beast blocks up the corridor
With monstrous hairy carcase, red and dun –
Too late: for I've sped through.

O Life! O Sun!

Goliath and David 1916

A Dead Boche

To you who'd read my songs of War
  And only hear of blood and fame,
I'll say (you've heard it said before)
  'War's Hell!' and if you doubt the same,
To-day I found in Mametz wood
A certain cure for lust of blood:

Where, propped against a shattered trunk,
  In a great mass of things unclean
Sat a dead Boche: he scowled and stunk
  With clothes and face a sodden green,
Big-bellied, spectacled, crop-haired,
Dribbling black blood from nose and beard.

Goliath and David 1916

Letter to S.S. from Mametz Wood

I never dreamed we'd meet that day
In our old haunts down Fricourt way,
Plotting such marvellous journeys there
For jolly old 'Après-la-guerre'.
Well, when it's over, first we'll meet
At Gweithdy Bach, my country seat
In Wales, a curious little shop
With two rooms and a roof on top,
A sort of Morlancourt-ish billet
That never needs a crowd to fill it.
But oh, the country round about!
The sort of view that makes you shout
For want of any better way
Of praising God: there's a blue bay
Shining in front, and on the right
Snowden and Hebog capped with white,
And lots of other jolly peaks
That you could wonder at for weeks,
With jag and spur and hump and cleft.
There's a grey castle on the left,
And back in the high hinterland
You'll see the grave of Shawn Knarlbrand
Who slew the savage Buffaloon
By the Nant-col one night in June,
And won his surname from the horn
Of this prodigious unicorn.
Beyond, where the two Rhinogs tower,
Rhinog Fach and Rhinog Fawr,
Close there after a four years' chase
From Thessaly and the woods of Thrace,
The beaten Dog-cat stood at bay
And growled and fought and passed away.
You'll see where mountain conies grapple
With prayer and creed in their rock chapel
Which Ben and Claire once built for them;
They call it Söar Bethlehem.
You'll see where in old Roman days,
Before Revivals changed our ways,
The Virgin 'scaped the Devil's grab,
Printing her foot on a stone slab
With five clear toe-marks; and you'll find

The fiendish thumbprint close behind.
You'll see where Math, Mathonwy's son,
Spoke with the wizard Gwydion
And bad him for South Wales set out
To steal that creature with the snout,
That new-discovered grunting beast
Divinely flavoured for the feast.
No traveller yet has hit upon
A wilder land than Meirion,
For desolate hills and tumbling stones,
Bogland and melody and old bones.
Fairies and ghosts are here galore,
And poetry most splendid, more
Than can be written with the pen
Or understood by common men.
In Gweithdy Bach we'll rest awhile,
We'll dress our wounds and learn to smile
With easier lips; we'll stretch our legs,
And live on bilberry tart and eggs,
And store up solar energy,
Basking in sunshine by the sea,
Until we feel a match once more
For *anything* but another war.
So then we'll kiss our families,
And sail away across the seas
(The God of Song protecting us)
To the great hills of Caucasus.
Robert will learn the local *bat*
For billeting and things like that,
If Siegfried learns the piccolo
To charm the people as we go.
The jolly peasants clad in furs
Will greet the Welch-ski officers
With open arms, and ere we pass
Will make us vocal with Kavasse.
In old Bagdad we'll call a halt
At the Sashuns' ancestral vault;
We'll catch the Persian rose-flowers' scent,
And understand what Omar meant.
Bitlis and Mush will know our faces,
Tiflis and Tomsk, and all such places.
Perhaps eventually we'll get
Among the Tartars of Thibet,

Hobnobbing with the Chungs and Mings,
And doing wild, tremendous things
In free adventure, quest and fight,
And God! what poetry we'll write!

Goliath and David 1916

Finland

Feet and faces tingle
   In that frore land:
Legs wobble and go wingle,
   You scarce can stand.

The skies are jewelled all around,
The ploughshare snaps in the iron ground,
The Finn with face like paper
And eyes like a lighted taper
Hurls his rough rune
At the wintry moon
And stamps to mark the tune.

Fairies and Fusiliers 1917

A Boy in Church

'Gabble-gabble, . . . brethren, . . . gabble-gabble!'
   My window frames forest and heather.
I hardly hear the tuneful babble,
   Not knowing nor much caring whether
The text is praise or exhortation,
Prayer or thanksgiving, or damnation.

Outside it blows wetter and wetter,
   The tossing trees never stay still.
I shift my elbows to catch better
   The full round sweep of heathered hill.
The tortured copse bends to and fro
   In silence like a shadow-show.

The parson's voice runs like a river
   Over smooth rocks. I like this church:
The pews are staid, they never shiver,
   They never bend or sway or lurch.
'Prayer,' says the kind voice, 'is a chain
That draws down Grace from Heaven again.'

I add the hymns up, over and over,
   Until there's not the least mistake.
Seven-seventy-one. (Look! there's a plover!
   It's gone!) Who's that Saint by the lake?
The red light from his mantle passes
Across the broad memorial brasses.

It's pleasant here for dreams and thinking,
   Lolling and letting reason nod,
With ugly serious people linking
   Sad prayers to a forgiving God....
But a dumb blast sets the trees swaying
With furious zeal like madmen praying.

Fairies and Fusiliers 1917

Sospan Fach (The Little Saucepan)

Four collier lads from Ebbw Vale
Took shelter from a shower of hail,
And there beneath a spreading tree
Attuned their mouths to harmony.

With smiling joy on every face
Two warbled tenor, two sang bass,
And while the leaves above them hissed with
Rough hail, they started 'Aberystwyth'.

Old Parry's hymn, triumphant, rich,
They changed through with even pitch,
Till at the end of their grand noise
I called: 'Give us the "Sospan" boys!'

Who knows a tune so soft, so strong,
So pitiful as that 'Saucepan' song
For exiled hope, despaired desire
Of lost souls for their cottage fire?

Then low at first with gathering sound
Rose their four voices, smooth and round,
Till back went Time: once more I stood
With Fusiliers in Mametz Wood.

Fierce burned the sun, yet cheeks were pale,
For ice hail they had leaden hail;
In that fine forest, green and big,
There stayed unbroken not one twig.

They sang, they swore, they plunged in haste,
Stumbling and shouting through the waste;
The little 'Saucepan' flamed on high,
Emblem of hope and ease gone by.

Rough pit-boys from the coaly South
They sang, even in the cannon's mouth;
Like Sunday's chapel, Monday's inn,
The death-trap sounded with their din.

The storm blows over, Sun comes out,
The choir breaks up with jest and shout,
With what relief I watch them part –
Another note would break my heart!

Reveille February 1919

Ghost Raddled

'Come, surly fellow, come! A song!'
  What, madmen? Sing to you?
Choose from the clouded tales of wrong
  And terror I bring to you.

9

Of a night so torn with cries,
  Honest men sleeping
Start awake with glaring eyes,
  Bone-chilled, flesh creeping.

Of spirits in the web hung room
  Up above the stable,
Groans, knockings in the gloom,
  The dancing table.

Of demons in the dry well
  That cheep and mutter,
Clanging of an unseen bell,
  Blood choking the gutter.

Of lust frightful, past belief,
  Lurking unforgotten,
Unrestrainable endless grief
  From breasts long rotten.

A song? What laughter or what song
  Can this house remember?
Do flowers and butterflies belong
  To a blind December?

The Owl May 1919

Loving Henry

Henry, Henry, do you love me?
Do I love you, Mary?
Oh, can you mean to liken me
To the aspen tree.
Whose leaves do shake and vary,
From white to green
And back again,
Shifting and contrary?

Henry, Henry, do you love me,
Do you love me truly?
Oh, Mary, must I say again
My love's a pain,
A torment most unruly?
It tosses me
Like a ship at sea
When the storm rages fully.

Henry, Henry, why do you love me?
Mary, dear, have pity!
I swear, of all the girls there are
Both near and far,
In country or in city,
There's none like you,
So kind, so true,
So wise, so brave, so pretty.

Land and Water May 1919

The Kiss

Are you shaken, are you stirred
    By a whisper of love,
Spell-bound to a word
    Does Time cease to move,
Till her calm grey eye
    Expands to as sky
And the clouds of her hair
    Like storms go by?

Then the lips that you have kissed
    Turn to frost and fire,
And a white-streaming mist
    Obscures desire:
So back to their birth
    Fade water, air, earth,
And the First Power moves
    Over void and dearth.

Is that Love? no, but Death,
    A passion, a shout,
The deep in-breath,
    The breath roaring out,
And once that is flown,
    You must lie alone,
Without hope, without life,
    Poor flesh, sad bone.

The Century July 1919

Song: One Hard Look

Small gnats that fly
In hot July
And lodge in sleeping ears,
Can rouse therein
A trumpet's din
With Day-of-Judgement fears.

Small mice at night
Can wake more fright
Than lions at midday.
An urchin small
Torments us all
Who tread his prickly way.

A straw will crack
The camel's back,
To die we need but sip,
So little sand
As fills the hand
Can stop a steaming ship.

One smile relieves
A heart that grieves
Though deadly sad it be,
And one hard look
Can close the book
That lovers love to see –

The Owl October 1919

A Frosty Night

Mother
Alice, dear, what ails you,
   Dazed and white and shaken?
Has the chill night numbed you?
   Is it fright you have taken?

Alice
Mother, I am very well,
   I felt never better,
Mother, do not hold me so,
   Let me write my letter.

Mother
Sweet, my dear, what ails you?

Alice
No, but I am well;
The night was cold and frosty,
There's no more to tell.

Mother
Ay, the night was frosty,
   Coldly gaped the moon,
Yet the birds seemed twittering
   Through green boughs of June.

Soft and thick the snow lay,
   Stars danced in the sky.
Not all the lambs of May-day
   Skip so bold and high.
Your feet were dancing, Alice,
   Seemed to dance on air,
You looked a ghost or angel
   In the starlight there.

Your eyes were frosted starlight,
Your heart fire and snow.
Who was it said, 'I love you'?

Alice
Mother, let me go!

Georgian Poetry November 1919

Rocky Acres

This is a wild land, country of my choice,
   With harsh craggy mountain, moor ample and bare.
Seldom in these acres is heard any voice
   But voice of cold water that runs here and there
   Through rocks and lank heather growing without care.
No mice in the heath run nor no birds cry
For fear of the dark speck that floats in the sky.

He soars and he hovers rocking on his wings,
   He scans his wide parish with a sharp eye,
He catches the trembling of small hidden things,
   He tears them in pieces, dropping from the sky:
   Tenderness and pity the land will deny,
Where life is but nourished from water and rock
A hardy adventure, full of fear and shock.

Time has never journeyed to this lost land,
   Crakeberries and heather bloom out of date,
The rocks jut, the streams flow singing on either hand,
   Careless if the season be early or late.
   The skies wander overhead, now blue, now slate:
Winter would be known by his cold cutting snow
If June did not borrow his armour also.

Yet this is my country beloved by me best,
   The first land that rose from Chaos and the Flood,
Nursing no fat valleys for comfort and rest,
Trampled by no hard hooves, stained with no blood.
   Bold immortal country whose hill tops have stood
Strongholds for the proud gods when on earth they go,
Terror for fat burghers in far plains below.

Georgian Poetry November 1919

The Cupboard

Mother
What's in that cupboard, Mary?

Mary
Which cupboard, mother dear?

Mother
The cupboard of red mahogany
  With handles shining clear.

Mary
That cupboard, dearest mother,
  With shining crystal handles?
There's nought inside but rags and jags
  And yellow tallow candles.

Mother
What's in that cupboard, Mary?

Mary
Which cupboard, mother mine?

Mother
That cupboard stands in your sunny chamber,
  The silver corners shine.

Mary
There's nothing there inside, mother,
  But wool and thread and flax,
And bits of faded silk and velvet,
  And candles of white wax.

Mother
What's in that cupboard, Mary?
  And this time tell me true.

Mary
White clothes for an unborn baby, mother,
  But what's the truth to you?

Georgian Poetry November 1919

Lost Love

His eyes are quickened so with grief,
He can watch a grass or leaf
Every instant grow; he can
Clearly through a flint wall see,
Or watch the startled spirit flee
From the throat of a dead man.
   Across two counties he can hear,
And catch your words before you speak
The woodlouse or the maggot's weak
Clamour rings in his sad ear;
And noise so slight it would surpass
Credence: – drinking sound of grass,
Worm talk, clashing jaws of moth
Chumbling holes in cloth:
The groan of ants who undertake
Gigantic loads for honour's sake,
Their sinews creak, their breath comes thin:
Whir of spiders when they spin,
And minute whispering, mumbling, sighs
Of idle grubs and flies.
   This man is quickened so with grief,
He wanders god-like or like thief
Inside and out, below, above,
Without relief seeking lost love.

Treasure Box 1919

Outlaws

Owls: they whinney down the night,
   Bats go zigzag by.
Ambushed in shadow out of sight
   The outlaws lie.

Old gods, shrunk to shadows, there
   In the wet woods they lurk,
Greedy of human stuff to snare
   In webs of murk.

Look up, else your eye must drown
   In a moving sea of black
Between the tree-tops, upside down
   Goes the sky-track.

Look up, else your feet will stray
   Towards that dim ambuscade,
Where spider-like they catch their prey
   In nets of shade.

For though creeds whirl away in dust,
   Faith fails and men forget,
These aged gods of fright and lust
   Cling to life yet.

Old gods almost dead, malign,
   Starved of their ancient dues,
Incense and fruit, fire, blood and wine
   And an unclean muse.

Banished to woods and a sickly moon,
   Shrunk to mere bogey things,
Who spoke with thunder once at noon
   To prostrate kings.

With thunder from an open sky
   To peasant, tyrant, priest,
Bowing in fear with a dazzled eye
   Towards the East.

Proud gods, humbled, sunk so low,
   Living with ghosts and ghouls,
And ghosts of ghosts and last year's snow
   And dead toadstools.

Country Sentiment March 1920

Vain and Careless

Lady, lovely lady,
    Careless and gay!
Once when a beggar called
    She gave her child away.

The beggar took the baby,
    Wrapped it in a shawl.
'Bring her back,' the lady said,
    'Next time you call.'

Hard by lived a vain man,
    So vain and so proud,
He walks on stilts
    To be seen by the crowd.

Up above the chimney pots,
    Tall as a mast,
And all the people ran about
    Shouting till he passed.

'A splendid match surely,'
    Neighbours saw it plain,
'Although she is so careless,
    Although he is so vain.'

But the lady played bobcherry,
    Did not see or care,
As the vain man went by her
    Aloft in the air.

This gentle-born couple
    Lived and died apart.
Water will not mix with oil,
    Nor vain with careless heart.

Country Sentiment March 1920

18

The Troll's Nosegay

A simple nosegay! was that much to ask?
   (Winter still gloomed, with scarce a bud yet showing).
He loved her ill, if he resigned the task.
   'Somewhere,' she cried, 'there must be blossom blowing.'
It seems my lady wept and the troll swore
   By Heaven he hated tears: he'd cure her spleen;
Where she had begged one flower, he'd shower fourscore,
A haystack bunch to amaze a China Queen.

Cold fog-drawn Lily, pale mist-magic Rose
   He conjured, and in a glassy cauldron set
   With elvish unsubstantial Mignonette
And such vague blooms as wandering dreams enclose.
   But she?
      Awed,
         Charmed to tears,
            Distracted,
               Yet –
Even yet, perhaps, a trifle piqued – who knows?

To-Day March 1920

Modernist Delvings (1921-1926)

By 1920, Graves had already shown signs that he was distancing himself from the Georgian style in order to concentrate on the self-inquiry and psychological probing which had been induced by his nightmarish war-neurosis. There was more than a change in the subject matter of Graves's poetry; accompanying the questioning and self-examination was a noticeable switch in style, from the descriptiveness of the Georgian tradition to the asceticism of his new phase. Indeed, in comparison with the ornate verse of Graves's early period, the poetry which he wrote from 1921 to 1926 appears modest and unadorned.

Perhaps most noticeable in the poems of this section are Graves's delvings into the workings of the mind which, in true Modernist tradition, contain echoes of Freudian self-analysis. Graves, who was ultimately to reject the label of Modernist, was clearly under the same spell as the early Modernists. His explorations into the psyche sought answers not only to questions about his own inner nature, but also about the human condition in general, a dilemma which is probably best exemplified by the poem 'Down'.

As he gradually tackled and laid aside certain aspects of his war neurosis, Graves attempted to move beyond purely personal considerations and to embrace metaphysical concerns. These ruminations were eventually to lead Graves to the teachings of the Indian philosopher Basanta Mallik, and to an acceptance of relativism. Poems such as 'Attercop' and 'The Bowl and the Rim' reflect Graves's new non-judgmental stance, his philosophy that there is no right or wrong, good or bad. But for someone as emotionally driven as Graves, this period of detachment could not last very long, and even before the American poet Laura Riding appeared to shatter his apathetic vision, shades of the author's natural subjectivity were creeping into poems such as 'Full Moon' and 'Children of Darkness'. Three particularly well-crafted poems in his most stimulating volume of the period, *Welchman's Hose*, are 'Alice', 'From our Ghostly Enemy' and 'The Clipped Stater', providing evidence that Graves could blend effectively the intellectual with the emotional well before the advent of Laura Riding.

MAJOR POETRY VOLUMES

The Pier-Glass	London: Secker, 1921
Whipperginny	London: Heinemann, 1923
Mock Beggar Hall	London: The Hogarth Press, 1924
Welchman's Hose	London: The Fleuron, 1925
Poems (1914-1926)	London: Heinemann, 1927

The Stake

Naseboro' held him guilty,
  Crowther took his part,
Who lies at the cross-roads,
  A stake through his heart.

21

Spring calls, and the stake answers
    Throwing out shoots;
The towns debate what life is this
    Sprung from such roots.

Naseboro' says 'A Upas Tree';
    'A Rose', says Crowther;
But April's here to declare it
    Neither one nor other.

Neither ill nor very fair,
    Rose nor Upas,
But an honest oak-tree,
    As its parent was.

A green-tufted oak-tree
    On the green wold,
Careless as the dead heart
    That the roots enfold.

London Mercury June 1920

The Pier-Glass

(To T.E. Lawrence, who helped me with it)

Lost manor where I walk continually
A ghost, while yet in woman's flesh and blood.
Up your broad stairs mounting with outspread fingers
And gliding steadfast down your corridors
I come by nightly custom to this room,
And even on sultry afternoons I come
Drawn by a thread of time-sunk memory.

Empty, unless for a huge bed of state
Shrouded with rusty curtains drooped awry
(A puppet theatre where malignant fancy
Peoples the wings with fear). At my right hand
A ravelled bell-pull hangs in readiness
To summon me from attic glooms above
Service of elder ghosts; here at my left

A sullen pier-glass cracked from side to side
Scorns to present the face as do new mirrors
With a lying flush, but shows it melancholy
And pale, as faces grow that look in mirrors.

Is here no life, nothing but the thin shadow
And blank foreboding, never a wainscote rat
Rasping a crust? Or at the window pane
No fly, no bluebottle, no starveling spider?
The windows frame a prospect of cold skies
Half-merged with sea, as at the first creation,
Abstract, confusing welter. Face about,
Peer rather in the glass once more, take note
Of self, the grey lips and long hair dishevelled,
Sleep-staring eyes. Ah, mirror, for Christ's love
Give me one token that there still abides
Remote, beyond this island mystery
So be it only this side Hope, somewhere,
In streams, on sun-warm mountain pasturage,
True life, natural breath; not this phantasma.

A rumour, scarcely yet to be reckoned sound,
But a pulse quicker or slower, then I know
My plea is granted; death prevails not yet.
For bees have swarmed behind in a close place
Pent up between this glass and the outer wall.
The combs are founded, the queen rules her court,
Bee-serjeants posted at the entrance chink
Are sampling each returning honey-cargo
With scrutinizing mouth and commentary,
Slow approbation, quick dissatisfaction.
Disquieting rhythm, that leads me home at last
From labyrinthine wandering. This new mood
Of judgment orders me my present duty,
To face again a problem strongly solved
In life gone by, but now again proposed
Out of due time for fresh deliberation.
Did not my answer please the Master's ear?
Yet, I'll stay obstinate. How went the question,
A paltry question set on the elements
Of love and the wronged lover's obligation?
Kill or forgive? Still does the bed ooze blood?
Let it drip down till every floor-plank rot!

Yet shall I answer, challenging the judgment: —
'*Kill, strike the blow again, spite what shall come.*'
'Kill, strike, again, again,' the bees in chorus hum.

Athenaeum June 1920

The Gnat

The shepherd Watkin heard an inner voice
Calling 'My creature, ho! be warned, be ready!'
Calling, 'The moment comes, therefore be ready!'
And a third time calling, 'Creature, be ready!'

This old poor man mistook the call, which sounded
Not for himself, but for his pensioner.
Now (truth or phantasy) the shepherd nourished
Fast in his brain, due earnings of transgression,
A creature like to that avenging fly
Once crept unseen in at King Herod's ear,
Tunnelling gradually inwards, upwards,
Heading for flowery pastures of the brain,
And battened on such grand, presumptuous fare
As grew him brazen claws and brazen hair
And wings of iron mail. Old Watkin felt
A like intruder channelling to and fro.
He cursed his day and sin done in past years,
Repentance choked, pride that outlawed his heart,
So that at night often in thunderous weather
Racked with the pain he'd start
From sleep, incontinently howling, leaping,
Striking his hoar head on the cottage walls,
Stamping his feet, dragging his hair by the roots.
He'd rouse the Gnat to anger, send it buzzing
Like a huge mill, scraping with metal claws
At his midpoint of being; forthwith tumble
With a great cry for Death to stoop and end him.

Now Watkin hears the voice and weeps for bliss,
The voice that warned 'Creature, the time is come.'
Merciful Death, was it Death, all his desire?
Promised of Heaven, and speedy? O Death, come!

Only for one thought must he make provision,
For honest Prinny, for old bob-tail Prinny.
Another master? Where? These hillside crofters
Were spiteful to their beasts and mercenary.
Prinny to such? No, Prinny too must die.
By his own hand, then? Murder! By what other?
No human hand should touch the sacrifice,
No human hand;
God's hand then, through his temporal minister.

Three times has Watkin in the morning early
When not a soul was rising, left his flock,
Come to the Minister's house through the cold mist,
Clicked at the latch and slowly moved the gate,
Faltered, held back and dared not enter in.
'Not this time, Prinny, we'll not rouse them yet,
To-morrow, surely, for our death is tokened,
My death and your death with small interval.
We meet in fields beyond; be sure of it, Prinny!'

On the next night
The busy Gnat, swollen to giant size,
Pent-up within the skull, knew certainly,
As a bird knows in the egg, his hour was come.
The thrice repeated call had given him summons...
    He must out, crack the shell, out, out!
He strains, claps his wing, arches his back,
Drives in his talons, out! out!

In the white anguish of this travail, Watkin
Hurls off his blankets, tears an axe from the nail
Batters the bed, hews table, splits the floor,
Hears Prinny whine at his feet, leaps, strikes again,
Strikes, yammering.
                        At that instant with a clatter
Noise of a bursting dam, a toppling wall,
Out flies the new-born creature from his mouth
And humming fearsomely like a huge engine,
Rackets about the room, smites the unseen
Glass of half-open windows, reels, recovers,
Soars out into the meadows, and is gone.

25

Silence prolonged to an age. Watkin still lives?
The hour of travail by the voice foretold
Brought no last throbbings of the dying Body
In child-birth of the Soul. Watkin still lives.

Labourer Watkin delves in the wet fields.
Did an old shepherd die that night with Prinny,
Die weeping with his head on the outraged corpse?
Oh, he's forgotten. A dead dream, a cloud.
Labourer Watkin delves, drowsily, numbly,
His harsh spade grates among the buried stones.

The Pier-Glass February 1921

Down

Downstairs a clock had chimed, two o'clock only.
Then outside from the hen-roost crowing came.
But why should Shift-wing call against the clock,
Three hours from dawn? The shutters click and knock,
And he remembers a sad superstition
Unfitting for the sick-bed – Turn aside,
Distract, divide, ponder the simple tales
That puzzled childhood; riddles, turn them over,
Half-riddles, answerless, the more intense! –
Lost bars of music tinkling with no sense
Recur, drowning uneasy superstition.

Mouth open, he was lying, this sick man,
And sinking all the while; how had he come
To sink? On better nights his dream went flying,
Dipping, sailing the pasture of his sleep,
But now, since clock and cock, had sunk him down
Through mattress, bed, floor, floors beneath, stairs, cellars,
Through deep foundations of the manse; still sinking
Through upturned earth. How had he cheated space
With inadvertent motion or word uttered
Of too-close-packed intelligence (such there are)
That he should penetrate with sliding ease,
Dense earth, compound of ages, granite ribs

26

And groins? Consider, there was some word uttered,
Some abracadabra – then like a stage-ghost,
Funereally with weeping, down, drowned, lost!

Oh, to be a child once more, sprawling at ease,
On warm turf of a ruined castle court.
Once he had dropped a stone between flat slabs
That mask the ancient well, mysteriously
Plunging his mind down with it. Hear it go
Rattling and rocketing down in secret void.
Count slowly one, two, three! and echoes rise
Fainter and fainter, merged in the gradual hum
Of bees and flies; only a thin draught rises
To chill the drowsy air; he for a while
Lay without spirit; until that floated back
From the deep waters. Oh, to renew now
The bliss of repossession, kindly sun
Forfeit for ever, and the scent of thyme!

Falling, falling! Light closed up behind him,
Now stunned by the violent subterrene flow
Of rivers, whirling down to hiss below
On the flame-axis of this terrible world;
Toppling upon their water-fall, O spirit...

The Pier-Glass February 1921

Return

The seven years' curse is ended now
That drove me forth from this kind land,
From mulberry-bough and apple bough
And gummy twings the west-wind shakes,
To drink the brine from crusted lakes
And grit my teeth on sand.

The load that from my shoulder slips
Straightway upon your own is tied,
You, too, shall scorch your finger-tips,
With scrabbling on the desert's face
Such thoughts I had for this green place,
Sent scapegoat for your pride.

27

Now for your cold, malicious brain
And most uncharitable, cold heart,
You, too, shall clank the seven years' chain
On sterile ground for all time curst
With famine's itch and flames of thirst,
The blank sky's counterpart.

Here, Robin on a tussock sits,
And Cuckoo with his call of hope
Cuckoos awhile, then off he flits,
While peals of dingle-dongle keep
Troop discipline among the sheep
That graze across the slope.

A brook from fields of gentle sun,
Through the glade his water heaves,
The falling cone would well-nigh stun
That squirrel wantonly lets drop,
When up he scampers to tree-top,
And dives among the green.

Yet, no, I ask a wider peace
Than peace your heart could comprehend,
More ample than my own release;
Go, be you loosed from your right fate,
Go with forgiveness and no hate;
Here let the story end.

The Pier-Glass February 1921

Song of Contrariety

Far away is close at hand,
  Close joined is far away,
Love might come at your command
  Yet will not stay.

At summons of your dream-despair
  She could not disobey,
But slid close down beside you there
  And complaisant lay.

28

Yet now her flesh and blood consent
    In waking hours of day,
Joy and passion both are spent,
    Fading clean away.

Is the presence empty air,
    Is the spectre clay,
That Love, lent substance by despair,
Wanes, and leaves you lonely there
    On the bridal day?

Outlook May 1921

On the Ridge
('Love in Barrenness')

Below the ridge a raven flew
And we heard the lost curlew
Mourning out of sight below
Mountain tops were touched with snow;
Even the long dividing plain
Showed no wealth of sheep or grain,
But fields of boulders lay like corn
And raven's croak was shepherd's horn
To slow cloud shadow strayed across
A pasture of thin heath and moss.
The North Wind rose; I saw him press
With lusty force against your dress,
Moulding your body's inward grace,
And streaming off from your set face,
So now no longer flesh and blood
But poised in marble thought you stood;
O wingless Victory, loved of men,
Who could withstand your triumph then?

Nation July 1921

29

Sullen Moods

Love, do not count your labour lost
    Though I turn sullen, grim, retired
Even at your side; my thought is crossed
    With fancies by old longings fired.

And when I answer you, some days
    Vaguely and wildly, do not fear
That my love goes forbidden ways
    Hating the laws that bind it here.

If I speak gruffly, this mood is
    Mere indignation at my own
Shortcomings, plagues, uncertainties;
    I forget the gentler tone.

You, now that you have come to be
    My one beginning, prime and end,
I count at last as wholly me,
    Lover no longer nor yet friend.

Friendship is flattery, though close hid;
    Must I then flatter my own mind?
And must (which laws of shame forbid)
    Blind love of you make self-love blind?

Do not repay me my own coin,
    The sharp rebuke, the frown, the groan;
But stir my memory to disjoin
    Your emanation from my own.

Help me to see you as before
    When overwhelmed and dead, almost,
I stumbled on that secret door
    Which saves the live man from the ghost.

Be once again the distant light,
    Promise of glory, not yet known
In full perfection – wasted quite
    When on my imperfection thrown.

London Mercury September 1921

Old Wives' Tales
('Mermaid, Dragon, Fiend')

Were the tales they told absurd,
　　Random tags for a child's ear?
Soon I mocked at all I heard,
　　Though with cause indeed for fear.

Of the mermaids' doleful game
　　In deep water I heard tell,
Of lofty dragons blowing flame,
　　Of the hornèd fiend of Hell.

Now I have met the mermaid kin
　　And find them bound by natural laws,
They have neither tail nor fin,
　　But are the deadlier for that cause.

Dragons have no darting tongues,
　　Teeth saw-edged nor rattling scales,
No fire issues from their lungs,
　　Poison has not slimed their tails.

But they are creatures of dark air,
　　Unsubstantial tossing forms,
Thunderclaps of man's despair
　　In mid whirl of mental storms.

And there's a true and only fiend
　　Worse than prophets prophesy,
Whose full powers to hurt are screened
　　Lest the race of man should die.

Ever in vain may courage plot
　　The dragon's death with shield and sword,
Or love abjure the mermaid grot,
　　Or faith be fixed in one blest word.

Mermaids will not be denied
　　Of our last enduring shame,
The dragon flaunts his unpierced hide,
　　The fiend makes laughter with God's Name.

London Mercury September 1921

The Lands of Whipperginny

('Heaven or Hell or the Lands of Whipperginny.' –
Nashe's *Jack Wilton*)

Come closer yet, sweet honeysuckle, my coney, O my Jinny,
    With a low sun gilding the bloom of the wood.
Be this Heaven, be it Hell, or the Lands of Whipperginny,
    It lies in a fairy lustre, it savours most good.

Then stern proud psalms from the chapel on the moors
    Waver in the night wind, their firm rhythm broken,
Lugubriously twisted to a howling of whores
    Or lent an airy glory too strange to be spoken.

Voices Autumn 1921

The Red Ribbon Dream

As I stood by the stair-head in the upper hall
    The rooms to left and right were locked as before.
    It was senseless to hammer at an unreal door
Painted on the plaster of a ten-foot wall.

There was half-light here, piled darkness beyond
    Rising up sheer as the mountain of Time,
    The blank rock-face that no thought can climb,
Girdled around with the Slough of Despond.

I stood quite dumb, sunk fast in the mire,
    Lonely as the first man, or the last man,
    Chilled to despair since evening began,
Dazed for the memory of a lost desire.

But a voice said 'Easily,' and a voice said 'Come!'
    Easily I followed with no thought of doubt,
    Turned to the right hand, and the way stretched out;
The ground held firmly; I was no more dumb.

For that was the place where I longed to be,
    And past all hope there the kind lamp shone,
    The carpet was holy that my feet were on,
And logs on the fire lay hissing for me.

The cushions were friendship and the chairs were love,
    Shaggy with love was the great wolf skin,
    The clock ticked 'Easily' as I entered in,
'Come,' called the bullfinch from his cage above.

Love went before me; it was shining now
    From the eyes of a girl by the window wall,
    Whose beauty I knew to be fate and all
By the thin red ribbon on her calm brow.

Then I was a hero and a bold boy
    Kissing the hand I had never yet kissed;
    I felt red ribbon like a snake twist
In my own thick hair, so I laughed for joy.

                    *

I stand by the stair-head in the upper hall;
    The rooms to the left and right are locked as before.
    Once I found entrance, but now never more,
And Time leans forward with his glassy wall.

New Republic March 1922

A False Report
(*'Angry Samson'*)

Are they blind, the lords of Gaza,
That each his fellow urges
'Samson the proud is pillow-smothered,'
They raise mock dirges?

Philistines and dullards,
Turn, look with amaze
At my foxes running in your cornfields
With their tails ablaze,

At bloody jawbone, at bees flitting
From the stark lion's hide:
At these, the gates of well-walled Gaza,
Clanking to my stride.

Whipperginny March 1923

Children of Darkness

('In their generation wiser than the children of Light.')

We spurred our parents to the kiss,
Though doubtfully they shrank from this –
Day had no courage to review
What lusty dark alone might do –
Then were we joined from their caress
In heat of midnight, one from two.

This night-seed knew no discontent,
In certitude his changings went;
Though there were veils about his face,
With forethought, even in that pent place,
Down towards the light his way he bent
To kingdoms of more ample space.

Was Day prime error, that regret
For darkness roars unstifled yet?
That in this freedom, by faith won,
Only acts of doubt are done?
That unveiled eyes with tears are wet,
They loathe to gaze upon the sun?

Whipperginny March 1923

The Bowl and Rim

The bearded rabbi, the meek friar,
  Linked by their ankles in one cell,
Through joint distress of dungeon mire
  Learned each to love his neighbour well.

When four years passed and five and six,
  When seven years brought them no release,
The Jew embraced the crucifix,
  The friar assumed phylacteries.

Then every Sunday, keeping score,
  And every Sabbath in this hymn
They reconciled an age-long war
  Between the platter's bowl and rim.

Together.
Man-like he lived, but God-like he died,
  All Hatred from His thought removed,
Imperfect until crucified,
  In crucifixion well-beloved.

The Friar.
If they did wrong, He too did wrong,
  (For Love admits no contraries)
In blind religion rooted strong
  Both Jesus and the Pharisees.

'Love all men as thyself,' said He.
  Said they, 'Be just with man or dog,'
'But only loathe a Pharisee,'
  'But crucify this demagogue.'

He died forgiving on the Tree
  To make amends for earlier spite,
They raised him up their God to be,
  And black with black accomplished white.

The Rabbi.
When He again descends on man
  As chief of Scribes and Pharisees,
With loathing for the Publican,
  The maimed and halt His enemies,

And when a not less formal fate
   Than Pilate's justice and the Rood,
His righteous angers expiate
   To make men think Him wholly good,

Then He again will have done wrong,
   If God be Love for every man,
For lewd and lettered, weak and strong,
   For Pharisee or Publican,

Together.
But like a God He will have died,
   All hatred from His thought removed,
Imperfect until crucified,
   In crucifixion well-beloved.

Whipperginny March 1923

Full Moon

As I walked out one harvest night
   About the stroke of One,
The Moon attained to her full height
   Stood beaming like the Sun.
She exorcised the ghostly wheat
To mute assent in Love's defeat
   Whose tryst had now begun.

The fields lay sick beneath my tread,
   A tedious owlet cried;
A nightingale above my head
   With this or that replied,
Like man and wife who nightly keep
Inconsequent debate in sleep
   As they dream side by side.

Your phantom wore the moon's cold mask,
   My phantom wore the same,
Forgetful of the feverish task
   In hope of which they came,

Each image held the other's eyes
And watched a grey distraction rise
    To cloud the eager flame.

To cloud the eager flame of love,
    To fog the shining gate:
They held the tyrannous queen above
    Sole mover of their fate;
They glared as marble statues glare
Across the tessellated stair,
    Or down the Halls of State.

And now cold earth was Arctic sea,
    Each breath came dagger keen;
Two bergs of glinting ice were we,
    The broad moon sailed between;
There swam the mermaids, tailed and finned,
And Love went by upon the wind
    As though it had not been.

Winter Owl November 1923

Attercop: the all-wise spider

James derided Walter,
Twisting him a halter
Of argument and synthesis,
'Hang yourself, Poet, in this.'
Walter, whistling on a reed
'Sweet Melancholy', took no heed;
He lolled against a finger-post,
Preening Fancy's pinion,
He summoned bogle, elf and ghost,
With other trivial sprites that most
Resent the sour dominion
Of James, renowned philosopher;
He clothed each airy minion
With cobwebs, with gossamer,
He bade them cast in bonfire flames
All the writings of this James,
To smoke with yon green rubbish, sir!

Myself, not bound by James' view,
Nor Walter's, in a vision saw these two
Like trapped and weakening flies
In toils of the same hoary net;
I seemed to hear ancestral cries,
Buzzing, 'To our All-Wise, Omnivorous
Attercop, glowering over us,
Whose table we have set
With blood and bones and sweat.'
These old cries echo plainly yet,
Though James sits calmer now,
Composed, with spectacles on brow,
Explaining why and how,
Telling on the fingers of his hands,
And seldom losing count, the strands
Of intricate silk entangling both his feet.
He points, 'Here this and that web meet,
Yet, I surmise,
A different combination might arise
If that or this worked otherwise.'
He ponders where the Primal Den can be,
He holds the web to have no finity,
And boldly adds, 'Attercop has no base
In any sure discoverable place,
Lost in his own complexities of lace;
A most capricious Beast
Whose tricks need not concern us in the least.
He's mad, or, possibly, long years deceased;
But this web serves as flooring for us flies.
Who disregards this web binding the skies,
That man himself denies.
The Web! Life! Liberty! All else is lies!'

Lyrical Walter cannot speak
Philosophy, nor use the same technique,
But listen to his natural-magic charm
Potent, as he thinks, for harm,
Against the tyrant Attercop.
   'Brush down the cobwebs from the cupboard-top
   With a long feather-mop
   Go, cheerily stride at dawn
   With careless feet about the lawn
   Breaking the threads of gossamer;

This, then, shall prove a token
Of Liberty, my sapient sir.
Attercop, whose proud name with hate be spoken,
His net, too, shall be broken.'

Mock Beggar Hall May 1924

From Our Ghostly Enemy

The fire was already white ash
   When the lamp went out,
And the clock at that signal stopped:
The man in the chair held his breath
   As if Death were about.

The moon shone bright as a lily
   On his books outspread.
He could read in that lily light:
'When you have endured your fill,
   Kill!' the book read.

The print being small for his eyes,
   To ease their strain
A hasty candle he lit,
Keeping the page with his thumb.
   'Come, those words again!'

But the book he held in his hand
   And the page he held
Spelt prayers for the sick and needy,
'By God, they are wanted here,'
   With fear his heart swelled.

'I know of an attic ghost,
   Of a cellar ghost,
And of one that stalks in the meadows,
But here's the spirit I dread,'
   He said, 'the most;

'Who, without voice or body,
    Distresses me much,
Twists the ill to holy, holy to ill.
Confuses me, out of reach
    Of speech or touch;

'Who works by moon or by noon,
    Threatening my life.
I am sick and needy indeed.'
He went then filled with despairs
    Upstairs to his wife.

He told her these things, adding
    'This morning alone,
Writing, I felt for a match-box:
It rose up into my hand,
    Understand, on its own.

'In the garden yesterday
    As I walked by the beds,
With the tail of my eye I caught
    "Death within twelve hours"
    Written in flowers' heads.'

She answered him, simple advice
    But new, he thought, and true.
'Husband, of this be sure,
That whom you fear the most,
    This ghost, fears you.

'Speak to the ghost and tell him,
    "Whoever you be,
Ghost, my anguish equals yours,
Let our cruelties therefore end.
    Your friend let me be."'

He spoke, and the ghost, who knew not
    How he plagued that man,
Ceased, and the lamp was lit again,
And the dumb clock ticked again,
    And the reign of peace began.

London Mercury December 1924

Alice

When that prime heroine of our nation, Alice,
Climbing courageously in through the Palace
Of Looking Glass, found it inhabited
By chessboard personages, white and red,
Involved in never-ending tournament,
She being of true philosophic bent,
Had long foreshadowed something of this kind,
Asking herself, 'Suppose I stood behind
And viewed the fireplace of Their drawing room
From hearthrug level, why must I assume
That what I'd see would need to correspond
With what I see now? And the rooms beyond,
Why should they pair with our rooms?'
                                        She was right.
An earlier Einstein whom the Laws of Light
And Euclid's beg-the-question fallacies
Could not convince: a master-mind was Alice's;
Moreover, uncontent with what she had done,
Alice decided to enlarge her fun,
Setting herself with proper British phlegm
And simple faith in simple stratagem
To learn the rules and moves and perfect them.
So prosperously there she settled down
That six moves only and she'd won her crown,
A triumph surely; but her greater feat
Was rounding these adventures off complete,
Accepting them, when safe returned again,
As queer but true, not merely in the main
True, but as true as anything you'd swear to,
Not worse or better than the life we are heir to,
The waking life which, but I can't say why,
We worship as the sole Reality;
For Alice though a child could understand
That neither did this chance-discovered land
Make nohow or contrariwise the clean
Dull round of mid-Victorian routine,
Nor did Victoria's golden rule extend
Where formal logic also comes; thereafter
Begins that lubberland of dream and laughter,
The red and white flower spangled hedge, the grass
Where Apuleius pastured his Gold Ass,

Where young Gargantua made full holiday;
But further from our heroine not to stray,
Let us observe with what uncommon sense,
Though a secure and easy reference
Between Red Queen and kitten could be found,
She made no false assumption on that ground
(A trap in which the scientist would fall),
That queens and kittens are identical.

Welchman's Hose September 1925

The Figure-Head
('*Death of a Farmer*')

'What caused the breakdown, do I think?
Undoubtedly,' the Ox cried, 'Drink,
That first of all the reason dims,
Then staggers trunk and limbs.'

At this the Ass informed the Cow,
'There's little hope for Master now.
Since Sunday night he's grown so weak
He scarce can sip or speak.

'But grief? Of us fourfooted, though
Our disillusion has dawned slow,
I doubt there's one can dare pretend
Grief at this dodderer's end.'

'He's done no good about the farm
These fifteen years, but plenty harm.
For all his use,' the old Ass said,
'He might have long been dead.

'Our hopeful forbears at his birth
Proclaimed the reign of Heaven on Earth.
Now Ox and Ass (you, sir, and I)
Confess that view a lie.

42

'Still, to ensure domestic peace,
We've taught the turkeys, ducks and geese
"He rules, he rules, serene and great,
Proof-armoured against fate."

"Granted," we've said, "he's no more seen
Tending fat sheep in pastures green,
Or scattering at the break of morn
Largesse, profuse, of corn.

"Master must be assumed to know
Where best his favours to bestow.
He has left us (caring for us still)
To cultivate free-will.

"Himself, from some grand inner room,
Directs the cowman, steward and groom,
Makes up his ledgers, page by page,
In joy or solemn rage.

"Our feeding and our water-time,
Our breeding and our slaughter-time,
The dyke, the hedge, the plough, the cart,
These thoughts lie next his heart."

'The simple birds believed this true,
What now, poor poultry, will they do,
Stunned with confusion, when the glum
Gloved undertakers come,

'Tilting the coffin past the pond,
The ricks, the clamps, the yard beyond,
Skirting the midden-heap with care,
Then out, they know not where?'

'And I deplore,' the Stallion said,
'The passing of this figure-head,
A farm-yard moving masterless
Alarms me, I confess.'

'Tut,' the Cow answered, 'when he's gone
They'll find that farm-life still goes on.
Routine, be sure, ran much the same
Long years before he came.

'Though interregna, history shows,
Are fruitful of alarms and blows,
New masters always seem supplied
In place of those who have died.

'True, the same headstone marks them all,
"His rise was better than his fall,"
But if this next reign too starts well....
Hush, now! the passing-bell!'

Welchman's Hose September 1925

Ovid in Defeat

The grammar of Love's Art
   Ovid still teaches
Grotesque in Pontic snows
   And bearskin breeches.[1]

'Let man be ploughshare,
   Woman his field;
Flatter, beguile, assault,
   And she must yield.

'Snatch the morning rose
   Fresh from the wayside,
Deflower it in haste
   Ere the dew be dried.'

Ovid instructs you how
   Neighbours' lands to plough;
'Love smacks the sweeter
   For a broken vow.'

Follows his conclusion
   Of which the gist is
The cold '*post coitum
   Homo tristis.*'

[1] Pellibus et sutis arcent mala frigora braccis.

44

Thereat despairing,
  Other Ovids hallow
Ploughshare in rust
  And field left fallow,

Or, since in Logic books
  Proposed they find,
'Where two ride together,
  One rides behind,'

This newer vision
  Of love's revealed,
Woman as the ploughshare,
  Man, her field.

Man as the plucked flower
  Trampled in mire,
When his unfair fair
  Has eased desire.

One sort of error
  Being no worse than other,
O, hug this news awhile
  My amorous brother,

That the wheel of Fortune
  May be turned complete,
Conflict, domination,
  Due defeat.

Afterwards, when you weary
  Of false analogy,
Offending both philosophy
  And physiology,

You shall see in woman
  Neither more nor less
Than you yourself demand
  As your soul's dress.

Thought, though not man's thought,
  Deeds, but her own,
Art, by no comparisons
  Shaken or thrown.

Plough then salutes plough
And rose greets rose:
While Ovid in toothache goes
Stamping through old snows.

Welchman's Hose September 1925

The Clipped Stater

He, Alexander, had been deified
By loud applause of the Macedonian phalanx,
By sullen groans of the wide worlds he had vanquished.
Who but a God could have so hacked down their pride?

He would not take a Goddess to his Throne
In the elder style, remembering those disasters
That Juno's jealous eye brought on her Consort.
Thaïs was fair; but he must hold his own.

Nor would he rank himself a common god
In fellowship with those of Ind or Egypt
Whom he had shamed: even to Jove his father
Paid scant respect (as Jove stole Saturn's Nod).

Now meditates, 'No land of all known lands
Has offered me resistance, none denies me
Infinite power, infinite thought and knowledge;
What now awaits the assurance of my hands?'

He weeps: the occasion, documented well,
Begins my now for the first time recorded
And philosophic tale of The Clipped Stater
(Though how it came to me, I must not tell).

Alexander, in a fever of mind,
Reasons, 'Omnipotence by its very nature
Is infinite possibility and purpose,
Which must embrace, *that it can be confined.*'

Then Finity is true Godhead's final test,
Nor does it shear the grandeur from Free Being;
'I must fulfil my self by self-destruction.'
The curious phrase renews his conquering zest.

He assumes man's flesh. Djinn catch him up and fly
To a land of yellow men beyond his knowledge,
And that he does not know them, he takes gladly
For surest proof he has put his godhead by.

In Macedonia shortly it is said
'Alexander, our God, has died of a fever:
Demi-gods parcel out his huge dominions.'
So Alexander, as God, is duly dead.

But Alexander the Man, whom yellow folk
Find roving naked, armed with a naked cutlass,
Has Death, which is the stranger's fate, excused him.
Joyfully he submits to the alien yoke.

He is enlisted for the frontier guard
With gaol-rogues and the press-gang's easy captures;
Where captains who have felt the Crown's displeasure,
But have thought suicide too direct and hard,

Teach him a new tongue and the soldier's trade,
To which the trade *he* taught has little likeness,
So that he glories in his limitations:
At every turn his hands and feet are stayed.

'Who was your father, friend?' He answers 'Jove,'
'His father?' 'Saturn.' 'And *his* father?' 'Chaos.'
'And *his*?' Thus Alexander loses honour:
Ten fathers is the least that a man should prove.

Stripes and bastinadoes, famine and thirst,
All these he suffers, never in resolution
Wavering, nor in his heart enquiring whether
God can be by his own confines accursed.

And he grows grey and eats his frugal rice;
Endures his watch on the fort's icy ramparts,
Staring across the uncouth wildernesses,
And cleans his leather and steel; and shakes the dice.

He will not dream Olympicly, nor stir
To enlarge himself with comforts or promotion,
Nor evade punishment when, sour of temper,
He has pulled the corporal's nose and called him 'cur.'

His comrades mutinously demand their pay.
'We have had none since the Emperor's Coronation.
At one gold piece a year there are fifteen owing.
One-third that sum would bribe us free,' say they.

The pay-sack came at length, when hope was cold,
But much reduced in bulk since the first issue
By the Royal Treasurer; and he, be certain,
Kept back a half of the silver and all the gold.

Every official hand had dipped in the sack,
And the frontier captains, themselves disappointed
Of long arrears, took every doit remaining,
But from good feelings put a trifle back.

Telling their men, 'since no pay has come through
We will advance from our too lavish purses
To every man of the guard, a piece of silver.
Let it be repaid when you have your overdue.'

The soldiers, grumbling but much gratified
By thoughts of a drink and a drab, accept the favour,
And Alexander, advancing to the pay-desk,
Salutes and takes his earnings with no pride.

The coin is bored, to string with the country's bronze
On a cord, one side is scraped to glassy smoothness
And the Head, clipped of its hair and neck, bears witness
That it had a broad, more generous mintage once.

And Alexander gazing at it then
Knows it well for a Silver Alexander
Coined from the bullion taken at Arbela.
How is it current among these slant-eyed men?

He stands in a troubled reverie of doubt
Till a whip stings his shoulders and a voice bellows,
'Are you dissatisfied, you scum of the ditches?'
So he salutes again and turns about.

But he cannot fathom what the event may mean.
Was his lost Empire, then, not all-embracing?
And how does the stater, though defaced, owe service
To a God that is as if he had never been?

Is he still God? No, truly. Then all he knows
Is, he must keep the course he has resolved on;
He spends the coin on a feast of fish and almonds
And back to the ramparts briskly enough he goes.

Welchman's Hose September 1925

The Laura Riding Period (1927-1942)

Critics of Graves's poetry have long debated the extent of Laura Riding's influence on his philosophy and poetry. Her advent in his life in 1926 was undoubtedly timely, for Graves was in need of certainty, a clear sense of poetic direction. What Riding offered him was a ready-made philosophy of life and poetry which was to liberate Graves from his cultural bonds with England and from that which England stood for in his mind. Many of the Riding-influenced poems of the couple's early association turn on the concept of freedom. Among Graves's earliest tributes to his newly discovered muse is 'Pygmalion to Galatea', in which the marble statue Galatea, brought to life by the artist's desire, promises to liberate his 'bonds of sullen flesh' and to release him so that he may reach a higher plane.

Riding was gradually to free Graves from the inconsequential (to her) realities of 'history', to the extent that he could dedicate his life to his art. Indeed, 'To the Reader Over my Shoulder' provided proof of the confidence which Riding had instilled in Graves, whose victory over fear of rejection by the reading public had liberated him from the dictates and expectations of 'pap-fed' readers and critics. Graves demonstrates in poems such as 'Front Door' that he was ready to reject family and cultural ties in order to be able to follow in the path of his liberator. The heart-felt dedicatory epilogue to Riding in *Good-bye To All That* (1929) is a tribute to her role in freeing Graves from 'politics, religion, conversations, literature, arguments, dances, drunks, time, crowds, games, fun, and unhappiness'.

For Riding, as she claimed in her *Collected Poems* Preface of 1938. a poem was 'an uncovering of truth', and in her view a firm dedication to this poetic purpose freed the poet from the temptations of the flesh and hence from an 'existence-in-time'. The best of Graves's poems written under Riding's tutelage – 'Ulysses', 'Certain Mercies', 'A Jealous Man', 'The Challenge' and the amusing 'Down, Wanton, Down' – are those in which Graves struggles with himself (almost always unsuccessfully) to match Riding's abstractions. These poems point to the tension between the emotional (Graves's natural poetic instinct) and the intellectual (Riding's conviction of the superiority of intellect over the senses).

Riding's sudden dismissal of Graves in 1939 might have caused emotional chaos at the time, but her departure with Schuyler Jackson forced him to re-assess his poetic vocation. Although during their years together she undoubtedly stifled certain aspects of his character, Riding led Graves to realize the complexities of love and the truth at the core of all relationships. The next few years after Riding's desertion were a difficult period of transition for Graves, but his faith in the power of love was to usher him towards an era in which the appreciation of a new kind of love was paramount: the period of the White Goddess.

MAJOR POETRY VOLUMES

Poems 1926-1930	London: Heinemann, 1931
Poems 1930-1933	London: Barker, 1933
Collected Poems 1938	London: Cassell, 1938

Pygmalion to Galatea

Pygmalion spoke and sang to Galatea
Who keeping to her pedestal in doubt
Of these new qualities, blood, bones and breath,
Nor yet relaxing her accustomed poise,
Her Parian rigour, though alive and burning,
Heard out his melody:

'As you are woman, so be lovely:
Fine hair afloat and eyes irradiate,
Long crafty fingers, fearless carriage,
And body lissom, neither small nor tall;
So be lovely!

'As you are lovely, so be merciful:
Yet must your mercy abstain from pity:
Prize your self-honour, leaving me with mine:
Love if you will: or stay stone-frozen.
So be merciful!

'As you are merciful, so be constant:
I ask not you should mask your comeliness,
Yet keep our love aloof and strange,
Keep it from gluttonous eyes, from stairway gossip,
So be constant!

'As you are constant, so be various:
Love comes to sloth without variety.
Within the limits of our fair-paved garden
Let fancy like a Proteus range and change.
So be various!

'As you are various, so be woman:
Graceful in going as well-armed in doing.
Be witty, kind, enduring, unsubjected:
Without you I keep heavy house.
So be woman!

'As you are woman, so be lovely:
As you are lovely, so be various,
Merciful as constant, constant as various.
So be mine, as I yours for ever.'

Then as the singing ceased and the lyre ceased,
Down stepped proud Galatea with a sigh.
'Pygmalion, as you woke me from the stone,
So shall I you from bonds of sullen flesh.
Lovely I am, merciful I shall prove:
Woman I am, constant as various,
Not marble-hearted but your own true love.
Give me an equal kiss, as I kiss you.'

London Mercury May 1926

The Taint

Being born of a dishonest mother
Who knew one thing and thought the other,
A father too whose golden touch
Was 'think small, please all, compass much'
He was hard put to it to unwind
The early swaddlings of his mind.

'Agree, it is better to confess
The occasion of my rottenness
Than in a desperation try
To cloak, dismiss or justify
The inward taint: of which I knew
Not much until I came to you
And saw it then, furred on the bone,
With as much horror as your own.

'You were born clean; and for the sake
Of your strict eyes I undertake
(If such disunion be allowed
To speak a sentence, to go proud
Among the miseries of to-day)
No more to let mere doing weigh
As counterbalance in my mind
To being rotten-boned and blind,
Nor leave the honesty and love
Of both only for you to prove.'

Harpers September 1926

Pure Death

This I admit, Death is terrible to me,
To no man more so, naturally,
And I have disenthralled my natural terror
Of every comfortable philosopher
Or tall dark doctor of divinity:
Death stands again in his true rank and order.

Therefore it was, when between you and me
Giving presents became a malady,
The exchange increasing surplus on each side
Till there was nothing but ungiveable pride
That was not over-given, and this degree
Called a conclusion not to be denied,

That we at last bethought ourselves, made shift
And simultaneously this final gift
Gave. Each with shaking hands unlocks
The sinister, long, brass-bound coffin-box,
Unwraps pure Death, with such bewilderment
As greeted our love's first accomplishment.

Nation November 1926

This Is Noon

You were with me last night and I with you,
But this is noon: do I dare swear it true
That love rose up in wrath to make us blind
And rapt from us all powers of heart and mind,
So we were maimed and had no pulse or thought
But love, love, love, in the one bale-fire caught?

You pass, you smile: yet is that smile I see
Of love, and of your all-night gift to me?
Now I too smile, for doubt, and own the doubt,
And wait in fear for night to root it out
And doubt the more; but take heart to be true,
Each time of change, to a fresh hope of you,

That love may find its proof once more and be
Fierce as it was last night in you and me,
For all it smiles at the blank dawn and soon
Is last night's dream of doubt and 'This is noon.'

Poems 1914-1926 June 1927

The Nape of the Neck

To speak of the hollow nape where the close chaplet
Of thought is bound, the loose-ends lying neat
In two strands downward, where the shoulders open
Casual and strong below, waiting their burden,
And the long spine begins its downward journey:
The hair curtains this postern silkily,
This secret stairway by which thought will come
More personally, with a closer welcome,
Than through the latticed eyes or portalled ears;
Where kisses and all unconsidered whispers
Go smoother in than by the very lip,
And more endeared because the head's asleep
Or grieving, the face covered with the hands.

'But equally,' you say, 'to these neck-ribbands —'

To be near napeless, headsunk, simian
Forgoes the privilege of man and woman.
The tighter bound the chaplet, the more easy
The door moves on its hinges; the more free
The stair, then the more sure the tenancy —

'But equally,' you say, 'to these neck-ribbands
May come one night the hypocrite assassin
With show of love or wisdom thrusting in
And, prompted in the watchword of the day,
Run up and stab and walk unseen away.'
But there's no need to use such melodrama,
For each betrayer only can betray
Once and the last effect of violation
Need be no ruin, no grief or contrition

55

(Despite tradition)
But a clear view: 'I was betrayed indeed,
Yet to a strictness and a present need.'
And it should come to this, to wear with pride
The knife scars that it would be shame to hide,
And once more without shuddering or hardness
Loll down the head to any chosen kiss.

Poems 1914-1926 June 1927

The Cool Web

Children are dumb to say how hot the day is,
How hot the scent is of the summer rose,
How dreadful the black wastes of evening sky,
How dreadful the tall soldiers drumming by.

But we have speech, that cools the hottest sun,
And speech that dulls the hottest rose's scent.
We spell away the overhanging night,
We spell away the soldiers and the fright.

There's a cool web of language winds us in,
Retreat from too much gladness, too much fear:
We grow sea-green at last and coldly die
In brininess and volubility.

But if we let our tongues lose self-possession,
Throwing off language and its wateriness
Before our death, instead of when death comes,
Facing the brightness of the children's day,
Facing the rose, the dark sky and the drums,
We shall go mad no doubt and die that way.

Poems 1914-1926 June 1927

Hell

Husks, rags and bones, waste paper, excrement
  Denied a soul whether for good or evil,
So casually consigned to unfulfilment,
  Are pronged into his bag by the great-devil.

And words repeated, over and over and over,
  Until their soul sickens and all but dies,
These the great-devil tenderly as a lover
  Will lay his hands upon and hypnotise.

From husks and rags and waste and excrement
  He forms the pavement-feet and the lift-faces;
He leads the sick words into parliament
  To rule a dust-bin world with deep-sleep phrases.

When living words and men meet, two and two
  In this one-twentieth part still actual scene,
They exchange pinches at their 'How d'ye do?'
  For a punctilious 'Do you mean what you mean?'

But to their table-converse boldly comes
  The same great-devil with his brush and tray,
To conjure plump loaves from the scattered crumbs,
  And feed his false five-thousands day by day.

Poems 1914-1927 1927

The Dead Ship
('Ship Master', later 'The Furious Voyage')

So, overmasterful, to sea!
But hope no distant view of sail,
No growling ice, nor weed, nor whale,
Nor breakers perilous on the lee.

Though you enlarge your angry mind
Three leagues and more about the ship
And stamp till every puncheon skip,
The wake runs evenly behind.

And it has width enough for you,
This vessel, dead from truck to keel
With an ignoble random wheel,
A blank chart and a surly crew,

In ballast only due to fetch
The turning-point of wretchedness
On an uncoasted featureless
And barren ocean of blue stretch.

London Mercury November 1927

Between Dark and Dark
('O Love in Me', later 'Sick Love')

O love, be fed with apples while you may
And feel the sun and go in royal array,
A smiling innocent on the heavenly causeway.

Though in what listening horror for the cry
That soars in outer blackness dismally,
The dumb blind beast, the paranoiac fury,

Be warm, enjoy the season, lift your head,
Exquisite in the pulse of tainted blood,
That shivering glory not to be despised.

Take your delight in momentariness,
Walk between dark and dark, a shining space
With the grave's narrowness, though not its peace.

Poems, 1929 December 1929

In Broken Images

He is quick, thinking in clear images;
I am slow, thinking in broken images.

He becomes dull, trusting to his clear images;
I become sharp, mistrusting my broken images.

Trusting his images, he assumes their relevance;
Mistrusting my images, I question their relevance.

Assuming their relevance, he assumes the fact,
Questioning their relevance, I question the fact.

When the fact fails him, he questions his senses;
When the fact fails me, I approve my senses.

He continues quick and dull in his clear images;
I continue slow and sharp in my broken images.

He in a new confusion of his understanding;
I in a new understanding of my confusion.

Poems, 1929 December 1929

To the Galleys
('Thief')

To the galleys, thief, and sweat your soul out
With strong tugging under the curled whips,
That their your thievishness may have full play.
Whereas, before, you stole rings, flowers and watches,
Oaths, jests and proverbs,
Yet paid for bed and board like an honest man,
This shall be entire thiefdom, you shall steal
Sleep from chain-galling, diet from soured crusts,
Comradeships from the damned, the ten-year chained,
And more than this, the excuse for life itself
From the galley steered toward battles not your own.

Poems, 1929 December 1929

Warning to Children

Children, if you dare to think
All the many largeness, smallness,
Fewness of this single only
Endless world in which you say
You live, you think of things like this: —
Lumps of slate enclosing dappled
Red and green, enclosing tawny
Yellow nets, enclosing white
And black acres of dominoes.
In the acres a brown paper
Parcel, then untie the string.
In the parcel a small island,
On the island a large tree,
On the tree a husky fruit,
Strip the husk and cut the rind off.
In the centre you will see
Lumps of slate enclosed by dappled
Red and green, enclosed by tawny
Yellow nets, enclosed by white
And black acres of dominoes.
In the acres a brown paper
Parcel, leave the string untied.
If you dare undo the parcel
You will find yourself inside it,
On the island, in the fruit,
With the parcel still untied,
Just like any lump of slate,
Find yourself enclosed by dappled
Green and red, enclosed by yellow
Tawny nets, enclosed by black
And white acres of dominoes.
And, children, if you dare to think
All the many largeness, smallness,
Fewness of this single only
Endless world in which you say
You live, you then untie the string.

Poems, 1929 December 1929

Against Kind

Become invisible by elimination
   Of kind in her, she none the less persisted
Among kind with no need to find excuses
   For choosing this and not some alien region.

Invisibility was her last kindness:
   She might have kept appearance, had she wished,
   Yet to be seen living against all kind
That would be monstrous; she permitted blindness.

She asked and she permitted nothing further,
   She went her private and eventless way
   As uncompanioning as uncompanioned,
So for a while they were not loth to lose her.

And yet it vexed them that her name still stood
   Plain on their registers, but over-simple,
   Unitemized by laundry, light or fuel,
Or even, they wondered most, by drink and food.

They tried omission; it was not for long:
   Pride and curiosity raised a whisper
   That swelled into a legend and the legend
Confirmed itself in terror and grew strong.

It was not that they would prefer her presence
   To her room (they hated her) but that her room
   Could not be filled by any creature of kind,
It gaped; they shook with sudden impotence.

Sleeplessness and shouting and new rumours
   Rummaged them nightly; grief perplexed their days;
   They waited for a sign, but none was given;
She owed them nothing, they held nothing of hers.

They raged at her that being invisible
   She would not use that gift, not humouring them
   As Lilith, or as an idiot poltergeist,
Or as a Gyges turning the ring's bezel.

She gave no sign; they therefore tumbled prostrate
   Fawning on her, confessing her their sins,
   They burned her the occasion's frankincense
Crying 'save, save!' but she was yet discrete.

And she must stay discrete, as they are blind
   For ever, or for one time less than ever
   If they, despaired and turning against kind,
Become invisible too, and read her mind.

Poems, 1929 December 1929

Midway

Between insufferable multiples
And as insufferable pauciples
Midway is man's convenience; we no longer
Need either hang our heads or lift them high
Unless for the weather's sake or when we dance.
We have a date neither with the fore-beings
Of Betelgeux nor with the atom's git.
The scale steadies; at this point we renew
Our fears of earthquakes, adders, floods, mad dogs
And all such wholesomes. Nothing that we do
Is quotable or is not to be quoted.
Clocks tick with our consent to our time-tables,
Trains run to our time-tables. Time and space
Once more distract us with their rough-house turn
Their hard head-on collision in the tunnel.
A necessary superstition groans
'Abide with me' and improvises God;
So history still is written and is read
By the unbelieving for the unremembering.

Poems, 1929 December 1929

Castle
('The Castle')

Walls, mounds, enclosing corrugations
Of darkness, moonlight on dry grass.
Walking this courtyard, sleepless, in fever,
Planning to use – but by definition
There's no way out, no way out –
Rope-ladders, baulks of timber, pulleys,
A rocket whizzing over the walls and moats –
Machines easy to improvise. No escape,
No such thing; to dream of new dimensions,
Cheating checkmate by painting the king's cheek
So that he slides like a queen.
Or to cry nightmare, nightmare,
Like a corpse in the cholera-pit
Under a load of corpses.
Or to run the head against these blind walls,
Enter the dungeon, torment the eyes.
With apparitions chained two and two,
And go frantic with fear,
And die and wake up seating in moonlight
In the same courtyard, sleepless as before.

Poems, 1929 December 1929

Front Door
('Front Door Soliloquy')

Since from the antique heights or deeps of that
Or this was grandeur fallen, sprung or that
Or this, beyond doubt I am grandeur's grandson
True to the eagle nose, the pillared neck,
(Missed by the intervening generation)
Whom large hands, long face and long feet sort out
From this and that, to wear my heels down even,
To be connected with all reigning houses,
Show sixteen quarterings or sixty-four,
Or even more, with clear skin and eyes clear
To drive the nails in without wounding wood,

63

With lungs and heart sound and with bowels easy,
An angry man, heaving the sacks of grain
From cart to loft and that and that and this
And even so, and being no Rousseauist,
Nor artists of the world unite, or this,
Or that, never admitting, in effect,
Touch anything my touch does not adorn –
Now then I dung on my grandfather's doorstep
Which is a reasonable and loving due
To hold no taint of love or vassalage
And understood only to him and me –
But you, you bogratwhiskered, mean, psalm-griddling,
Lame, rotten-livered, this and that canaille,
You, when twin lacqueys, with armorial shovels,
Unbolt the bossy gates and bend to the task,
Keep well behind the railings, if you must watch,
Lest they mistake you this for that you are.

Poems, 1929 December 1929

Landscape
('Nature's Lineaments')

When mountain rocks and leafy trees
And clouds and things like these,
With edges,

Caricature the human face,
Such scribblings have no grace
Or peace –

The bulbous nose, the sunken chin,
The ragged mouth in grin
Of cretin.

Nature is always so, you find
That brutal-comic mind,
As wind,

Retching among the empty spaces,
Ruffling the idiot grasses,
The sheep's fleeces.

Whose pleasures are excreting, poking,
Havocking and sucking,
Sleepy licking.

Whose griefs are melancholy,
Whose flowers are oafish,
Whose waters, silly,
Whose birds, raffish,
Whose fish, fish.

Poems, 1929 December 1929

Sandhills
('Sea Side')

Into a gentle wildness and confusion,
Of here and there, of one and everyone,
Of windy sand-hills by an unkempt sea,
Came two with two in search of symmetry,
Found symmetry of two in sea and sand,
In left foot, right foot, left hand and right hand.

The beast with two backs is a single beast,
Yet by his love of singleness increased
By two and two and two and two again
Until instead of sandhills is a plain
Disposed in two and two, by two and two,
And the sea parts in horror at the view.
Rather an antique Three (beard, beard and bird,
Or three old spinning women, spinning hard)
Than two-four-eight-sixteenish single same
Re-registration of the duple name.

Poems, 1929 December 1929

Quayside
('A Former Attachment')

And glad to find, on again looking at it;
It was not nearly so good as I had thought –
You know the ship is moving when you see
The boxes on the quayside sliding away
And growing smaller – and having real delight
When the port's cleared and the coast out of sight,
And ships are few, each on its proper course,
With no occasion for approach or discourse.

Poems, 1929 December 1929

It Was All Very Tidy

When I reached his place,
The grass was smooth,
The wind was delicate,
The wit well-timed,
The limbs well-formed,
The pictures straight on the wall.
It was all very tidy.

He was cancelling out
The last row of figures,
He had his beard tied up in ribbons,
There was no dust on his shoe,
Everyone laughed.
It was all very tidy.

Music was not playing,
There were no sudden noises,
The sun shone blandly,
The clock ticked.
It was all very tidy.

'Apart from and above all this,'
I reassured myself,
'Am I not myself?'
It was all very tidy.

Death did not address me,
He had nearly done.
It was all very tidy.

They asked, did I consent
It was all very tidy?

I could not bring myself,
For shame, to untie
His beard's neat ribbons,
Or jog his elbow,
Or whistle and sing,
Or make disaster.
I consented, fearfully,
He was not unwelcome.
It was all very tidy.

Poems, 1929 December 1929

Interruption

If ever against this easy blue and silver
Hazed-over countryside of thoughtfulness
Far behind in the mind and above,
Boots from before and below approach tramping,
Watch how their premonition will display
A forward countryside, low in the distance,
A picture-postcard square of June grass,
Will warm a summer season, trim the hedges,
Cast the river about on either flank,
Start the late cuckoo emptily calling,
Invent a rambling tale of moles and voles,
Furnish a path with stiles.
Watch how the field will broaden, the feet nearing,
Sprout with great dandelions and buttercups,
Widen and heighten. The blue and silver
Fogs at the border of this all-grass.
Interruption looms gigantified,
Lurches against, treads thundering through,
Blots the landscape, scatters all,
Roars and rumbles like a dark tunnel,
Is gone.

The picture-postcard grass and trees
Swim back to central: it is a large patch,
It is a modest, failing patch of green,
The postage-stamp of its departure,
Clouded with blue and silver, closing in now
To a plain countryside of less and less,
Unpeopled and unfeatured blue and silver,
Before, behind, above.

Ten Poems More June 1930

The Age of Certainty
('New Legends')

Content in you,
Andromeda alone,
Yet queen of air and ocean
And every fiery dragon,
Chained to no cliff,
Asking no rescue of me.

Content in you,
Mad Atalanta
Stooping unpausing
Ever ahead
Acquitting me of rivalry.

Content in you,
Invariable she-Proteus
Sole unrecordable
Giving my tablets holiday.

Content in you,
Niobe of no children
Sorrow no calamity.

Content in you,
Helen, foiler of beauty.

Ten Poems More June 1930

The Beast (I)
('Saint')

Edmund Spenser loathed the Blatant Beast,
Yet to the history's end withheld the stroke
That must, he knew, provoke
Rancour in men that loved the monster least.

And this was prudence: while the Beast lives
The infamy of his ravage is delight
And to the Red Cross Knight
A fore-won laurel of salvation gives.

But the Beast killed is carrion and a worse
Than carrion: which old Spenser would not tell
Knowing his Faerie well —
Therefore to me it falls to write that curse.

This foul Beast, then, was finally overcome
And in no secret combat: the whole city
Flocked out and groaned for pity
To see the Red Cross Knight urge the blade home.

Duly they danced, and sang the triumphs due,
Roasting whole oxen on the public spit;
Twelve mountain peaks were lit
With bonfires: yet their hearts were doubt and rue.

Therefore no grave was deep enough to hold
The Beast, which after days came thrusting out,
Wormy from rump to snout,
His draggled cere-cloth foul with the grave's mould.

Nor could sea hold him: anchored with great stones
He swelled and buoyed them up, paddling to shore
As evident as before
With deep-sea ooze and salty creaking bones.

Lime could not burn him, nor the hot coal-fire:
So often as the good Knight bound him there,
With stink of singeing hair
And scorching flesh the corpse rolled from the pyre.

In the city-gutter would the Beast lie
Praising the Knight for his high valorous deeds:
'Ay, on those water-meads
He slew even me. These death-wounds testify.'

The Knight governed that city, a man shamed
And shrunken; for the Beast was over-dead,
With wounds no longer red
But gangrenous and loathsome and inflamed.

Not all the righteous judgements he could utter,
Nor mild laws frame, nor public works repair,
Nor wars wage, in despair,
Could bury that same Beast, crouched in the gutter.

A fresh remembrance-banquet to forestall
The Knight turned hermit, went without farewell
To a far mountain-cell:
But the Beast followed as his seneschal,
And there drew water for him and hewed wood
With vacant howling laughter; else all day
Noisome with long decay
Sunning himself at the cave's entry stood.

He would bawl to pilgrims for a dole of bread
To feed the sick saint who once vanquished him
With spear so stark and grim:
Would set a pillow of grass beneath his head,
Would fetch him fever-wort from the pool's brim;
And crept into his grave when he was dead.

Ten Poems More June 1930

The Terraced Valley

In a deep thought of you and concentration
I came by hazard to a strange region:
The unnecessary sun was not there,
The necessary earth was without care,
Broad sunshine ripened the whole skin
Of ancient earth that was turned outside-in.

Calm sea beyond the terraced valley
Without horizon easily was spread
As it were overhead
Washing the mountain-spurs behind me:
The unnecessary sky was not there,
Therefore no heights, no deeps, no birds of the air.

Neat outside-inside, neat below-above
Hermaphrodising love.
Neat this-way-that-way and without mistake:
On the right hand could slide the left glove.
Neat over-under: the young snake
Through an unbreaking shell his path could break.
Singing of kettles, like a singing brook,
Made out of doors a fireside nook.

But you, my love, where had you then your station?
Seeing that on this common earth together
We go not distant from each other
I knew you near me in that strange region,
So searched for you, in hope to see you stand
On some near olive-terrace, in the heat,
The left-hand glove drawn on your right hand,
The empty snake's egg perfect at your feet –

But found you nowhere in the whole land,
And cried disconsolately, until you spoke
Close in the sunshine by me, and your voice broke
That antique spell with a doom-echoing shout
To once more inside-in and outside-out.

Ten Poems More June 1930

Act V Scene 5

'You choose the old nurse and the little page
To act survivors on your tragic stage,
Each an unnecessary player.'
'No, not unnecessary,' you say; 'if none
Survive to moralise on what's been done
This is no tragedy, but dead men's laughter.
Tears are the purge – the nurse's broken line
"O mistress, pretty one, dead!" the page's whine
"Thou too? Alas, fond master!"

'No purge for my complaint: I'd have them own
Small sorrow to be left on-stage alone
And in the bloodiest royal massacre
Either rant out the anti-climax well:
"'A's dead, the bitch!" "So's Oscar: snug in Hell!" –
Then fall to rifling pocket, belt and purse
With corky jokes in character,
Or, drive the feud yet further: page with nurse
His jewelled dirk against her sooty cleaver.'

Ten Poems More June 1930

Tail Piece: a song to make you and me laugh
('Lift Boy', later 'Song: Lift-Boy', eventually 'Lift-Boy')

Let me tell you the story of how I began:
I began as the knife-boy and ended as the boot-man,
With nothing in my pockets but a jack-knife and a button,
With nothing in my pockets but a jack-knife and a button,
    With nothing in my pockets.

Let me tell you the story of how I went on:
I began as the lift-boy and ended as the lift-man,
With nothing in my pockets but a jack-knife and a button,
With nothing in my pockets but a jack-knife and a button,
    With nothing in my pockets.

I found it very easy to whistle and play
With nothing in my head or my pockets all day,
With nothing in my pockets.

But along came Old Eagle, like Moses or David,
He stopped me at the fourth floor and preached me Damnatio⌐
'Not a soul shall be savèd, not one shall be savèd.
The whole First Creation shall forfeit salvation:
From knife-boy to lift-boy, from ragged to regal,
Not one shall be savèd, not you, nor Old Eagle,
No soul on earth escapeth, even if all repent —'
So I cut the cords of the lift and down we went,
With nothing in our pockets.

Can a phonograph lie? Can a phonograph lie?
Can a, can a phonograph?
A song very neatly
Contrived to make you and me
Laugh.

Ten Poems More June 19

Brother

It is odd enough to be alive with others,
But odder yet to have sisters and brothers,
To make one with a characteristic litter —
The sister doubtful and vexed, the brothers vexed and bitter
That this one wears, through praise and through abuse
His family nose for individual use.

Poems 1926-1930 February 19

Flying Crooked

The butterfly, the cabbage-white,
(His honest idiocy of flight)
Will never now, it is too late,
Master the art of flying straight,
Yet has – who knows so well as I? –
A just sense of how not to fly:
He lurches here and here by guess
And God and hope and hopelessness.
Even the aerobatic swift
Has not his flying-crooked gift.

Poems 1926-1930 February 1931

The Felloe'd Year

The pleasure of summer was its calm success
Over winter past and winter sequent;
The pleasure of winter was a warm counting,
'Summer comes again, when, surely'.
This pleasure and that pleasure touched
In a perpetual spring-with-autumn ache,
A creak and groan of season,
In which all move,
In which all move yet, samely, but not I
For whom the twelve spokes of the felloe'd year
Are the fixed compass, not the turning wheel.

To Whom Else July 1931

On Time
('Time')

The vague sea thuds against the marble cliffs
And from their fragments age-long grinds
Pebbles like flowers.

Or the vague weather wanders in the fields,
When up spring flowers with coloured buds
Like marble pebbles.

The beauty of the flowers is time, death-grieved;
The pebbles' beauty too is time,
Life-weary.

It is all too easy to admire a flower
Or a smooth pebble flower-like freaked
By time and vagueness.

Time is the lie of lies: sweet oil that eases
All obstinate locks and rusty hinges
With loving-kindness.

Time is old age and crafty childhood, both:
What monster lives heart-whole against
His innocent vagueness,

Or will not render him the accustomed tax,
Humouring age with filial flowers,
Childhood with pebbles?

To Whom Else July 1931

To Whom Else?

To whom else other than,
To whom else not of man
Yet in human state,
Standing neither in stead
Of self nor idle godhead,
Should I, man in man ended,
Myself dedicate?

To whom else momently,
To whom else endlessly,
But to you, I?
To you who only,
To you who mercilessly,
To you who lovingly,
Plucked out the lie?

To whom else less acquaint,
To whom else without taint
Of death, death-true?
With great astonishment
Thankfully I consent
To my estrangement
From me in you.

To Whom Else July 1931

On Portents

If strange things happen where she is,
So that men say that graves open
And the dead walk, or that futurity
Becomes a womb and the unborn are shed,
Such portents are not to be wondered at
Being tourbillions in Time made
By the strong pulling of her bladed mind
Through that ever-reluctant element.

To Whom Else July 1931

The Bards
('Lust in Song')

Their cheeks are blotched for shame, their running verse
Stumbles, with marrow-bones the drunken diners
Pelt them as they delay:
It is a something fearful in the song
Plagues them, an unknown grief that like a churl
Goes common-place in cowskin
And bursts unheralded, crowing and coughing,
An unpilled holly-club twirled in his hand,
Into their many-shielded, samite-curtained
Jewel-bright hall where twelve kings sit at chess
Over the white-bronze pieces and the gold,
And by a gross enchantment

Flails down the rafters and leads off the queens –
The wild-swan-breasted, the rose-ruddy-cheeked
Raven-haired daughters of their admiration –
To stir his black pots and to bed on straw.

Poems 1930-1933 May 1933

Ulysses

To this much-tossed Ulysses never done
   With woman, whether in the gown of wife or whore,
Penelope and Circe seemed as one:
She like a whore made his lewd fancies run
   And wifely she a hero to him bore.

Their counter-changings terrified his way:
   They were the clashing rocks, Symplegades,
Scylla and Charybdis too were they;
Now they were the storms frosting the sea with spray
   And now the Lotus Orchard's filthy ease.

They multiplied into the Sirens' throng,
   Forewarned by fear of whom he stood bound fast
Hand and foot helpless at the vessel's mast,
Yet would not stop his ears, daring their song:
   He gasped and sweated till that shore was past.

One, two and many: flesh had made him blind.
   Flesh had one pleasure only in the act,
Flesh set one purpose only in the mind –
Triumph of flesh and the continuance kind
   Of those same terrors with which flesh was racked.

His wiles were pleasant and his fame far known:
   Every king's daughter sought him for her own.
Yet he was nothing to be won or lost.
All lands to him were Ithaca: love-tossed
   He loathed the fraud, yet would not bed alone.

Poems 1930-1933 May 1933

Down, Wanton, Down!

Down, wanton, down! Have you no shame
That at the whisper of Love's name
Or Beauty's, presto! up you raise
Your angry head and stand at gaze?

Poor bombard-captain, sworn to reach
The ravelin and effect a breach,
Indifferent what you storm or why
So be that in the breach you die!

Love may be blind, but Love at least
Knows what is man and what mere beast:
Or beauty, wayward, but requires
More delicacy from her squires.

Tell me, my witless, whose one boast
Could be your staunchness at the post,
When were you made a man of parts
To think fine and profess the arts?

Will many-gifted Beauty come
Bowing to your bald rule of thumb,
Or Love swear loyalty to your crown?
Be gone, have done! Down, wanton, down!

Poems 1930-1933 May 1933

The Cell
('The Philosopher')

Three blank walls, a barred window with no view,
A ceiling within reach of the raised hands,
A floor blank as the walls.

But ruling out distractions of the body —
Growth of the hair and nails, a prison diet,
Thoughts of escape,

Ruling out memory and fantasy,
The distant tramping of the gaoler's boots,
Visiting mice and such,

What refuge here for a laborious mind!
What a redoubtable and single task
Could one attempt here:

Threading connexion between wall and wall
And floor and ceiling, more attentively
Than the cob-spider –

Plain logic without benefit of flies –
Spinning and knotting till the cell became
A spacious other head

In which the emancipated reason might
Learn in due time to walk more accurately
And neatly than at home.

Poems 1930-1933 May 1933

Nobody

Nobody, ancient mischief, nobody
Harasses always with an absent body.

Nobody coming up the road, nobody,
Like a tall man in a dark cloak, nobody.

Nobody about in the house, nobody,
Like children creeping up the stairs, nobody.

Nobody anywhere in the garden, nobody,
Like a young girl quiet with needlework, nobody.

Nobody coming, nobody, not yet here,
Incessantly welcomed by the wakeful ear.

Until this nobody shall consent to die
Under his curse must every man lie –

The curse of his jealousy, of his grief and fright,
Of sudden rape and murder screamed in the night.

Poems 1930-1933 May 1933

Danegeld

When I ceased to be a child
   I had great discontent
With a not-me unreconciled
   To what I thought and meant.

Some told me this, or that, or this –
   No counsel was the same:
Some preached God's holy purposes,
   Some used the Devil's name.

I made my truce with foreignness,
   As seemed the easiest plan:
The curious hauntings should express
   A me complete as man.

But this enlargement only spelt
   To see and yet be blind –
A pirate flesh allowed Danegeld
   By an unready mind.

Had I but held my truth apart
   And granted greed no say
In what I saw, deep in my heart,
   Must be my body way!

Poems 1930-1933 May 1933

The Climate of Thought

The climate of thought has seldom been described.
It is no terror of Caucasian frost,
Nor yet that brooding Hindu heat
For which a loin-rag and a dish of rice
Suffice until the pestilent monsoon.
But, without winter, blood would run too thin;
Or, without summer, fires would burn too long.
In thought the seasons run concurrently.

Thought has a sea to gaze, not voyage on;
Mountains, to rough the edge of the bland sky,
Not to be climbed in search of blander prospect;
Few birds, sufficient for such caterpillars
As are not fated to turn butterflies;
Few butterflies, sufficient for the flowers
That are the luxury of a full orchard;
Wind, sometimes, in the evening chimneys; rain
On the early morning roof and on the sight;
Snow streaked upon the mountain, feeding
The fond brook at the valley-head
That greens the valley and that parts the lips;
The sun, simple, like a country neighbour;
The moon, grand, not fanciful with clouds.

Epiloque II July 1936

A Jealous Man

To be homeless is a pride
To the jealous man prowling
Hungry down the night lanes,

Who has no steel at his side,
No drink hot in his mouth,
But a mind dream-enlarged,

Who witnesses warfare,
Man with woman, hugely
Raging from hedge to hedge:

81

The raw knotted oak-club
Clenched in the raw fist,
The ivy-noose well flung,

The thronged din of battle,
Gaspings of the throat-snared
Snores of the battered dying,

Tall corpses, braced together,
Fallen in clammy furrows,
Male and female,

Or, among haulms of nettle
Humped, in noisome heaps,
Male and female.

Who glowers in the choked roadway
Between twin churchyards,
Like a turnip ghost.

(Here, the rain-worn headstone,
There, the Celtic cross
In rank white marble.)

This jealous man is smitten,
His fear-jerked forehead
Sweats a fine musk;

A score of bats bewitched
By the ruttish odour
Swoop singing at his head;

Nuns bricked up alive
Within the neighbouring wall
Wail in cat-like longing.

Crow, cocks, crow loud!
Reprieve the doomed devil,
Has he not died enough?

Now, out of careless sleep,
She wakes and greets him coldly,
The woman at home,

She, with private wonder
At shoes bemired and bloody –
His war was not hers.

Epiloque II July 1936

Never Such Love

Twined together and, as is customary,
For words of rapture groping, they
'Never such love,' swore, 'ever before was.'
Contrast with all loves that had failed or staled
Registered their own as love indeed.

And was this not to blab idly
The heart's fated inconstancy?
Better in love to seal the love-sure lips,
For truly love was before words were,
And no word given, no word broken.

When more than 'love!' is uttered
(Love, the near-honourable malady
With which in greed and haste they
Each other did infect and curse)
Or, worse, is written down....

Wise after the event, by love withered,
Their 'never more!' most frantically
A grief and shame did proclaim
Such as they swore, never before was:
True lovers even in this.

Epiloque II July 1936

To Walk on Hills

To walk on hills is to employ legs
As porters of the head and heart
Jointly adventuring towards
Perhaps true equanimity.

To walk on hills is to see sights
And hear sounds unfamiliar.
When in wind the pine-tree roars,
When crags with bleatings echo,
When water foams below the fall,
Heart records that journey
As memorable indeed;
Head reserves opinion,
Confused by the wind.

A view of three shires and the sea!
Seldom so much at once appears
Of the coloured world, says heart.
Head is glum, says nothing.
Legs become weary, halting
To sprawl in a rock's shelter,
While the sun drowsily blinks
On head at last brought low –
This giddied passenger of legs
That has no word to utter.

Heart does double duty,
As heart, and as head,
With portentous trifling.
A castle on its crag perched
Across the miles between is viewed
With awe as across years.

Now a daisy pleases,
Pleases and astounds, even,
That on a garden lawn could blow
All summer long with no esteem.

And the buzzard's horrid poise,
And the plover's misery,
And the important beetle's
Blue-green-shiny black...

To walk on hills is to employ legs
To march away and lose the day.
Confess, have you known shepherds?
And are they not a witless race
Prone to quaint visions?
Not thus from solitude
(Solitude sobers only)
But from long hilltop striding.

Epiloque II July 1936

The Exile
('The Cloak')

Into exile with only a few shirts,
Some gold coin and the necessary papers.
But winds are contrary: the Channel packet
Time after time returns the sea-sick peer
To Sandwich, Deal or Rye. He does not land,
But keeps his cabin; so at last we find him
In humble lodging at perhaps Dieppe,
His shirts unpacked, his night-cap on a peg,
Passing the day with cards and swordsmanship
Or merry passages with chambermaids,
By night at his old work. And all is well –
The country wine wholesome although so sharp,
And French his second tongue; a faithful valet
Brushes his hat and brings him newspapers.
This nobleman is at home anywhere,
His castle being, the valet says, his title.
The cares of an estate would incommode
Such tasks as now his Lordship has in hand.
His Lordship, says the valet, contemplates
A profitable absence of some years.
Has he no friend at Court to intercede?
He wants none: exile's but another name
For an old habit of non-residence
In all but the recesses of his cloak.
It was this angered a great personage.

Epiloque III April 1937

End of Play

We have reached the end of pastime, for always,
Ourselves and everyone, though few confess it
Or see the sky other than, as of old,
A foolish smiling Mary-mantle blue;

Though life may still seem to dawdle golden
In some June landscape among sleepy flowers,
The grass to shine as cruelly green as ever,
Faith to descend in a chariot from the sun.

May seem only: a mirror and an echo
Mediate henceforth with vision and sound.
The cry of faith, no longer frolicsome,
Sounds as a blind man's pitiful plea of 'blind'.

We have at last ceased idling, which to regret
Were as shallow as to ask our milk teeth back;
As many forthwith do, and on their knees
Call lugubriously upon chaste Christ.

We tell no lies now, at last we cannot be
The rogues we were – so evilly linked in sense
With what we scrutinized that lion or tiger
Could leap from every copse, strike and devour us.

No more shall love in hypocritic pomp
Conduct its innocents through a dance of shame
From the first touching of gloved finger tips
To frantic laceration of naked breasts.

Yet love survives, the word carved on a sill
Under antique dread of the headsman's axe;
It is the echoing mind, as in the mirror
We stare on our dazed trunks at the block kneeling.

Epiloque III April 1937

86

Parent to Children

When you grow up, are no more children,
Nor am I then your parent:
The day of settlement falls.

'Parent', mortality's reminder,
In each son's mouth or daughter's
A word of shame or rage!

I who begot you ask no pardon of you;
Nor may the soldier ask
Pardon of the strewn dead.

The procreative act was blind:
It was not you I sired then —
For who sires friends, as you are mine now?

Yet I envisaged progeny,
And children I begot, to fear;
And these were you, though now are not you.

In fear begotten, I begot in fear.
Would you have had me cast fear out
So that you should not be?

And will you be revenged,
Filially name me
Grandparent to your children — tree of fear?

Or, bolder than I was,
Scorn the consanguine vice,
Reject all loves born of bed-ignorance?

Epiloque III April 1937

Certain Mercies

Now must all satisfaction
Become mere mitigation
Of an accepted curse?

Must we henceforth be grateful
That the guards, though spiteful,
Are slow of foot and wit?

That by night we may spread
Over the plank bed
A thin coverlet?

That the rusty water
In the unclean pitcher
Our thirst quenches?

That the rotten, detestable
Food is yet eatable
By us ravenous?

That the prison censor
Permits a weekly letter?
(We may write: 'we are well.')

That with patience and deference
We do not experience
The punishment cell?

That each new indignity
Defeats only the body,
Pampering the spirit
With obscure, proud merit?

Collected Poems 1938 November 1938

The Cuirassiers of the Frontier

Goths, Vandals, Huns, Isaurian mountaineers,
Made Roman by our Roman sacrament,
We can know little (as we care little)
Of the Metropolis: her candled churches,
Her white-gowned pederastic senators,
The cut-throat factions of her Hippodrome,
The eunuchs of her draped saloons.

Here is the frontier, here our camp and place –
Beans for the pot, fodder for horses,
And Roman arms. Enough. He who among us
At full gallop, the bowstring to his ear,
Lets drive his heavy arrows, to sink
Stinging through Persian corslets damascened,
Then follows with the lance – he has our love.

The Christ bade Holy Peter sheathe his sword,
Being outnumbered by the Temple guard.
And this was prudence, the cause not yet lost
While Peter might persuade the crowd to rescue.
Peter renegued, breaking his sacrament.
With us the penalty is death by stoning,
Not to be made a bishop.

In Peter's Church there is no faith nor truth,
Nor justice anywhere in palace or court.
That we continue watchful on the rampart
Concerns no priest. A gaping silken dragon,
Puffed by the wind, suffices us for God.
We, not the City, are the Empire's soul:
A rotten tree lives only in its rind.

Collected Poems 1938 November 1938

Hotel Bed
('Hotel Bed at Lugano')

Even in hotel beds the hair tousles.
But this is observation, not complaint –
'Complaints should please be dropped in the complaint-box' –
'Which courteously we beg you to vacate
In that clean state as you should wish to find it.'

And the day after Carnival, to-day,
I found, in the Square, a crimson cardboard heart:
'Anna Maria,' it read. Otherwise, friends,
No foreign news – unless that here they drink
Red wine from china bowls; here anis-roots
Are stewed like turnips; here funiculars
Light up at dusk, two crooked constellations. . . .

'It is not yet the season,' pleads the Porter,
'That comes in April, when the rain most rains.'
Trilingual Switzer fish in Switzer lakes
Pining for rain and bread-crumbs of the season,
In thin reed-beds you pine!

                              In bed drowsing,
(While the hair slowly tousles) uncomplaining. . . .
Anna Maria's heart under my pillow
Evokes no furious dreams. Who is this Anna?
A Switzer maiden among Switzer maidens,
Child of the children of that fox who never
Ate the sour grapes: her teeth not set on edge.

Collected Poems 1938 November 1938

Leda

Heart, with what lonely fears you ached,
    How lecherously mused upon
That horror with which Leda quaked
    Under the spread wings of the swan.

Then soon your mad religious smile
　　Made taut the belly, arched the breast,
And there beneath your god awhile
　　You strained and gulped your beastliest.

Pregnant you are, as Leda was,
　　Of bawdry, murder and deceit;
Perpetuating night because
　　Stale after-languors hang so sweet.

Collected Poems 1938 November 1938

Recalling War

Entrance and exit wounds are silvered clean,
The track aches only when the rain reminds.
The one-legged man forgets his leg of wood,
The one-armed man his jointed wooden arm.
The blinded man sees with his ears and hands
As much or more than once with both his eyes.
Their war was fought these twenty years ago
And now assumes the nature-look of time,
As when the morning traveller turns and views
His wild night-stumbling carved into a hill.

What, then, was war? No mere discord of flags
But an infection of the common sky
That sagged ominously upon the earth
Even when the season was the airiest May.
Down pressed the sky and we, oppressed, thrust out
Boastful tongue, clenched fist and valiant yard.
Natural infirmities were out of mode,
For Death was young again: patron alone
Of healthy dying, premature fate-spasm.

Fear made fine bed-fellows. Sick with delight
At life's discovered transitoriness,
Our youth became all-flesh and waived the mind.
Never was such antiqueness of romance,
Such tasteless honey oozing from the heart.
And old importances came swimming back –

Wine, meat, log-fires, a roof over the head,
A weapon at the thigh, surgeons at call.
Even there was a use again for God –
A word of rage in lack of meat, wine, fire,
In ache of wounds beyond all surgeoning.

War was return of earth to ugly earth,
War was foundering of sublimities,
Extinction of each happy art and faith
By which the world had still kept head in air,
Protesting logic or protesting love,
Until the unendurable moment struck –
The inward scream, the duty to run mad.

And we recall the merry ways of guns –
Nibbling the walls of factory and church
Like a child, piecrust; felling groves of trees
Like a child, dandelions with a switch!
Machine-guns rattle toy-like from a hill,
Down in a row the brave tin-soldiers fall:
A sight to be recalled in elder days
When learnedly the future we devote
To yet more boastful visions of despair.

Collected Poems 1938 November 1938

To Evoke Posterity

To evoke posterity
Is to weep on your own grave,
Ventriloquizing for the unborn:
'Would you were present in flesh, hero,
What wreaths and junketings!'

And the punishment is known:
To be found fully ancestral,
To be cast in bronze for a city square,
To dribble green in times of rain
And stain the pedestal.

Spiders in the spread beard;
A life proverbial
On clergy lips a-cackle;
Eponymous institutes,
Their luckless architecture.

Two more dates of life and birth
For the hour of special study
From which all boys and girls of mettle
Twice a week play truant
And worn excuses try.

Alive, you have abhorred
The crowds on holiday
Jostling and whistling – yet you would air
Your death-mask, smoothly lidded,
Along the promenade?

Collected Poems 1938 November 1938

Defeat of the Rebels

The enemy forces are in wild flight.
Poor souls (you say), they were intoxicated
With rhetoric and banners, thought it enough
To believe and to blow trumpets, to wear
That menacing lie in their shakos.

Enough: it falls to us to shoot them down,
The incorrigibles and cowards,
Where they shiver behind rocks or in ditches
Seek graves that have no headstones to them –
Such prisoners were unprofitable.

Now as our vanguard, pressing on,
Dislodges them from village and town,
Who yelling abandon packs and cloaks,
Their arms and even the day's rations,
We are not abashed by victory,

We raise no pitying monument
To check the counter-stroke of fortune.
These are not spoils: we recognize
Our own strewn gear, that never had been robbed
But for our sloth and hesitancy.

Collected Poems 1938 November 1938

The China Plate

From a crowded barrow in a street-market
The plate was ransomed for a few coppers,
Was brought gleefully home, given a place
On a commanding shelf.

'Quite a museum-piece,' an expert cries
(Eyeing it through the ready pocket-lens) —
As though a glass case would be less sepulchral
Than the barrow-hearse!

For weeks this plate retells the history
Whenever an eye runs in that direction:
'Near perdition I was, in a street-market
With rags and old shoes.'

'A few coppers' — here once again
The purchaser's proud hand lifts down
The bargain, displays the pot-bank sign
Scrawled raggedly underneath.

Enough, permit the treasure to forget
The emotion of that providential purchase,
Becoming a good citizen of the house
Like its fellow-crockery.

Let it dispense sandwiches at a party
And not be noticed in the drunken buzz,
Or little cakes at afternoon tea
When cakes are in demand.

94

Let it regain a lost habit of life,
Foreseeing death in honourable breakage
Somewhere between the kitchen and the shelf –
To be sincerely mourned.

Collected Poems 1938 November 1938

The Halls of Bedlam

Forewarned of madness:
In three days' time at dusk
The fit masters him.

How to endure those days?
(Forewarned is foremad)
'– Normally, normally.'

He will gossip with children,
Argue with elders,
Check the cash account.

'I shall go mad that day –'
The gossip, the argument,
The neat marginal entry.

His case is not uncommon,
The doctors pronounce;
But prescribe no cure.

To be mad is not easy,
Will earn him no money,
But a niche in the news.

Then to-morrow, children,
To-morrow or the next day
He resigns from the firm.

His boyhood's ambition
Was to become an artist –
Like any City man's.

To the walls and halls of Bedlam
The artist is welcome –
Bold brush and full palette.

Through the cell's grating
He will watch his children
To and from school.

'Suffer the little children
To come unto me
With their Florentine hair!'

A very special story
For their very special friends –
They burst in the telling:

Of an evil thing, armed,
Tap-tapping on the door,
Tap-tapping on the floor,
'On the third day at dusk.'

Father in his shirt-sleeves
Flourishing a hatchet –
Run, children, run!

No one could stop him,
No one understood;
And in the evening papers....

(Imminent genius,
Troubles at the office,
Normally, normally,
As if already mad.)

Collected Poems 1938 November 1938

A Country Mansion

This ancient house so notable
For its gables and great staircase,
Its mulberry-trees and alleys of clipped yew,
Humbles the show of every near domain.

At the beginning it acknowledged owners –
Father, son, grandson –
But then, surviving the last heirs of the line,
Became a place for life-tenancy only.

At the beginning, no hint of fate,
No rats and no hauntings;
In the garden, then, the fruit-trees grew
Slender and similar in long rows.

A bedroom with a low ceiling
Caused little fret at first;
But gradual generations of discomfort
Have bred an anger there to stifle sleep.

And the venerable dining-room,
Where port in Limerick glasses
Glows twice as red reflected
In the memory-mirror of the waxed table –

For a time with paint and flowered paper
A mistress tamed its walls,
But pious antiquarian hands, groping,
Rediscovered the grey panels beneath.

Children love the old house tearfully,
And the parterres, how fertile!
Married couples under the testers hugging
Enjoy an antique bliss as nowhere else.

A smell of mould from loft to cellar,
Yet sap still brisk in the oak
Of the great beams: if ever they use a saw
It will stain, as cutting a branch from a green tree.

... Old Parr had lived one hundred years and five
(So to King Charles he bragged)
When he did open penance, in a sheet,
For fornication with posterity.

Old Parr died; not so this mansion
Whose inhabitants, bewitched,
Pour their fresh blood through its historic veins
And, if a tile blow from the roof, tremble.

The last-born of this race of sacristans
Broke the long spell, departed;
They lay his knife and fork at every meal
And every evening warm his bed;

Yet cannot draw him back from the far roads
For trifling by the lily-pool
Or wine at the hushed table where they meet,
The guests of genealogy.

It was his childhood's pleasure-ground
And still may claim his corpse,
Yet foster-cradle or foster-grave
He will not count as home.

This rebel does not hate the house,
Nor its dusty joys impugn:
No place less reverend could provoke
So proud an absence from it.

He has that new malaise of time:
Gratitude choking with vexation
That he should opulently inherit
The goods and titles of the extinct.

Collected Poems 1938 November 1938

The Eremites

We may well wonder at those froward hermits
Who like the scorpion and the basilisk
Crouched in the desert sands, to undo
Their scurfy flesh with tortures.

They drank from pools fouled by the ass and camel,
Chewed uncooked millet pounded between stones,
Wore but a shame-rag, dusk or dawn,
And rolled in thorny places.

In the wilderness there are no women;
Yet hermits harbour in their shrunken loins
A penitential paradise
A leaping-house of glory.

Solomons of a thousand lusty love-chants,
These goatish men, burned Aethiopian black,
Kept vigil till the angelic whores
Should lift the latch of pleasure.

And what Atellan orgies of the soul
Were celebrated then among the rocks
They testify themselves in books
That rouse Atellan laughter.

Haled back at last to wear the ring and mitre,
They clipped their beards and, for their stomachs' sake,
Drank now and then a little wine,
And tasted cakes and honey.

Observe then how they disciplined the daughters
Of noble widows, who must fast and thirst,
Abjure down-pillows, rouge and curls,
Deform their delicate bodies:

Whose dreams were curiously beset by visions
Of stinking hermits in a wilderness
Pressing unnatural lusts on them
Until they wakened screaming.

Such was the virtue of our pious fathers:
To refine pleasure in the hungry dream.
Pity for them, but pity too for us –
Our beds by their leave lain in.

Collected Poems 1938 November 1938

The Ages of Oath

To find a garden-tulip growing
Among wild primroses of a wild field,
Or a cuckoo's egg in a blackbird's nest,
Or a giant mushroom, a whole basketful –
The memorable feats of childhood!
Once, by the earthwork, scratching in the soil,
My stick turned up a Roman amber bead....

The lost, the freakish, the unspelt
Drew me: for simple sights I had no eye.
And did I swear allegiance then
To wildness, not (as I thought) to truth –
Become a virtuoso, and this also,
At last, of simple sights, when tiring
Of unicorn and upas?

Did I forget how to greet plainly
The especial sight, how to know deeply
The pleasure shared by many hearts?
And is this to begin afresh, with oaths
On the right book, in the right name,
Then stammering out my praise of you,
Like a boy owning his first love?

Collected Poems 1938 November 1938

The Fallen Tower of Siloam

Should the building totter, run for an archway!
We were there already – already the collapse
Powdered the air with chalk, and shrieking
Of old men crushed under the fallen beams
Dwindled to comic yelps. How not terrible
When the event outran the alarm
And suddenly we were free –

Free to forget how grim it stood,
That tower, and what great fissures ran
Up the west wall, how rotten the under-pinning
At the south-eastern angle. Satire
Had whirled a gentle wind around it,
As if to buttress the worn masonry;
Yet we, waiting, had abstained from satire.

It behoved us, indeed, as poets
To be silent in Siloam, to foretell
No visible calamity. Though kings
Were crowned and gold coin minted still and horses
Still munched at nose-bags in the public streets,
All such sad emblems were to be condoned:
An old wives' tale, not ours.

Collected Poems 1938 November 1938

The Great-Grandmother

That aged woman with the bass voice
And yellowing white hair: believe her.
Though to your grandfather, her son, she lied
And to your father disingenuously
Told half the tale as the whole,
Yet she was honest with herself,
Knew disclosure was not yet due,
Knows it is due now.

She will conceal nothing of consequence
From you, her great-grandchildren
(So distant the relationship,
So near her term),
Will tell you frankly, she has waited
Only for your sincere indifference
To exorcize that filial regard
Which has estranged her, seventy years,
From the folk of her house.

Confessions of old distaste
For music, sighs and roses –
Their false-innocence assaulting her,
Breaching her hard heart;
Of the pleasures of a full purse,
Of clean brass and clean linen,
Of being alone at last;
Disgust with the ailing poor
To whom she was bountiful;
How the prattle of young children
Vexed more than if they whined;
How she preferred cats.

She will say, yes, she acted well,
Took such pride in the art
That none of them suspected, even,
Her wrathful irony
In doing what they asked
Better than they could ask it...
But, ah, how grudgingly her will returned
After the severance of each navel-cord,
And fled how far again,
When again she was kind!

She has outlasted all man-uses,
As was her first resolve:
Happy and idle like a port
After the sea's recession,
She does not misconceive the nature
Of shipmen or of ships.
Hear her, therefore, as the latest voice;
The intervening generations (drifting
On tides of fancy still) ignore.

Collected Poems 1938 November 1938

No More Ghosts

The patriarchal bed with four posts
Which was a harbourage of ghosts
Is hauled out from the attic glooms
And cut to wholesome furniture for wholesome rooms;

Where they (the ghosts) confused, abused, thinned,
Forgetful how they sighed and sinned,
Cannot disturb our ordered ease
Except as summer dust tickles the nose to sneeze.

We are restored to simple days, are free
From cramps of dark necessity,
And one another recognize
By an immediate love that signals at our eyes.

No new ghost can appear. Their poor cause
Was that time freezes, and time thaws;
But here only such loves can last
As do not ride upon the weathers of the past.

Collected Poems 1938 November 1938

A Love Story

The full moon easterly rising, furious,
Against a winter sky ragged with red;
The hedges high in snow and owls raving –
Solemnities not easy to withstand:
A shiver wakes the spine.

In boyhood, having encountered the scene,
I suffered horror: I fetched the moon home,
With owls and snow, to nurse in my head
Throughout the trials of a new spring,
Famine unassuaged.

But fell in love, and made a lodgement
Of love on those frozen ramparts.
Her image was my ensign: snows melted,
Hedges sprouted, the moon tenderly shone,
The owls trilled with tongues of nightingale.

These were all lies, though they matched the time,
And brought me less than luck: her image
Warped in the weather, turned beldamish.
Then back came winter on me at a bound,
The pallid sky heaved with a moon-quake.

Dangerous it had been with love-notes
To serenade Queen Famine.
In tears I recomposed the former scene,
Let the snow lie, watched the moon rise, suffered the owls,
Paid homage to them of unevent.

No More Ghosts September 1940

To Sleep

The mind's eye sees as the heart mirrors:
Loving in part, I did not see you whole,
Grew flesh-enraged that I could not conjure
A whole you to attend my fever-fit
In the doubtful hour between a night and day
And be Sleep that had been so long away.

Of you sometimes a hand, a brooch, a shoe
Wavered beside me unarticulated –
As the vexed insomniac dream-forges;
And the words I chose for your voice to speak
Echoed my own voice with its dry creak.

Now that I love you, now that I recall
All scattered elements of will that swooped
By night as jealous dreams through windows
To circle above the beds like bats,
Or as dawn birds flew blindly at the panes
In curiosity rattling out their brains –

Now that I love you, as not before,
Now you can be and say, as not before,
The mind clears and the heart true-mirrors you
Where at my side an early watch you keep
And all self-bruising heads loll into sleep.

No More Ghosts September 1940

Under the White Goddess (1943-1959)

Graves made his initial discovery of the White Goddess during the research for his novel *Hercules, My Shipmate* (1944). The many references to the mother-goddess in the legends of heroes from a variety of cultural and religious sources generated in him such interest and excitement that by the end of the same year he had written the first full draft of *The White Goddess*.

Graves's goddess, 'a lovely, slender woman with a hooked nose, deathly pale face, lips red as rowan-berries, startlingly blue eyes, and long fair hair', became for him the muse of poetry, to whom he would dedicate his craft and from whom he would derive his poetic images. From Graves's point of view, a poet had to strive to excel in his inventiveness when writing of and for the muse-figure, his source of inspiration; should the muse fail to inspire, however, the poet would die a metaphorical death. It was the cruelty of the muse-figure, her feminine treachery etched out in the prototypes of Swinburnian pain-givers and Keatsian *belles dames*, that challenged the loyalty of her servants. For Graves, the test of his devotion and the reward of poetic inspiration were the essential elements of his art during this period.

Almost all of Graves's poetry written during the White Goddess phase was created in celebration of the muse-figure. In 'To Juan at the Winter Solstice', Graves outlines to his newborn son the grim fate that awaits those who devote themselves to the service of the muse, and in 'The White Goddess', her unworldly beauty encourages the poet to sacrifice himself for a glimpse of her radiance. 'Darien' illustrates the suffering which the poet must endure in the hope of being symbolically reborn under the muse's aegis. These themes are part of the 'one story and the one story only' which Graves was continually to recount throughout this period. Occasionally, as in 'The Destroyer', the theme focuses on those men who deny the goddess's power; in less didactic and more personal poems such as 'She Tells her Love while Half Asleep', 'The Portrait', and 'Counting the Beats', the reader appears to gain some respite from the omnipresent muse-figure, only to find her lurking in the guise of another alluring female, or in the figure of nature itself.

MAJOR POETRY VOLUMES:

Work in Hand	London: The Hogarth Press, 1942
Poems 1938-1945	London: Cassell, 1946
Collected Poems (1914-1947)	London: Cassell, 1948
Poems and Satires	London: Cassell, 1951
Poems 1953	London: Cassell, 1953
Collected Poems 1959	London: Cassell, 1959

Dawn Bombardment

Guns from the sea open against us:
The smoke rocks bodily in the casemate
And a yell of doom goes up.
We count and bless each new, heavy concussion –
Captives awaiting rescue.

Visiting angel of the wild-fire hair
Who in dream reassured us nightly
Where we lay fettered,
Laugh at us, as we wake – our faces
So tense with hope the tears run down.

Work in Hand March 1942

The Worms of History

On the eighth day God died: his bearded mouth
That had been shut so long flew open.
So Adam's too in a dismay like death –
But the world still rolled on around him,
Instinct with all those lesser powers of life
That God had groaned against but not annulled.

'All-excellent,' Adam had titled God,
And in his mourning now demeaned himself
As if all excellence, not God, had died;
Chose to be governed by those lesser powers,
More than inferior to excellence –
The worms astir in God's corrupt flesh.

God died, not excellence his name:
Excellence lived but only was not God.
It was those lesser powers who played at God,
Bloated with Adam's deferential sighs
Which were his mourning for divinity:
They reigned as royal monsters on the earth.

Adam grew lean, and wore perpetual black;
He made no reaching after excellence.
Eve gave him sorry comfort for his grief
With birth of sons, and mourning still he died.
Adam was buried in one grave with God
And the worms ranged and ravaged in between.

Into their white maws fell abundance
Of all things rotten. They were greedy-nosed
To smell the taint out and go scavenging,
Yet over excellence held no domain.
Excellence lives; they are already dead –
The ages of a putrefying corpse.

Work in Hand March 1942

The Shot

The curious heart plays with its fears:
To hurl a shot through the ship's planks,
Being assured that the green angry flood
Is charmed, it dares not dance into the hold –
Nor first to sweep a lingering glance around
For land or shoal or cask adrift.
'So miracles are done; but madmen drown.'

O weary luxury of hypothesis –
For human nature, honest human nature
(Which the fear-pampered heart denies)
Knows its own miracle: not to go mad.
Will pitch the shot in fancy, hint the fact,
Will bore perhaps a meagre auger hole
But stanch the spurting with a tarred rag,
And will not drown, nor even ride the cask.

Work in Hand March 1942

107

Lollocks

By sloth on sorrow fathered
These dusty-featured Lollocks
Have their nativity in all disordered
Backs of cupboard drawers.

They hide and seek
Among collars and novels
And empty medicine bottles,
And letters from abroad
That never will be answered.

Every sultry night
They plague little children,
Gurgling from the cistern,
Humming from the air,
Skewing up the bed-clothes,
Twitching the blind.

When the imbecile agèd
And over-long in dying
And the nurse drowses,
Lollocks come skipping
Up the tattered stairs
And are nasty together
In the bed's shadow.

The signs of their presence
Are boils on the neck,
Dreams of vexation suddenly recalled
In the middle of the morning,
Languor after food.

Men cannot see them,
Men cannot hear them,
Do not believe in them –
But suffer the more,
Both in neck and belly.

Women can see them –
O those naughty wives
Who sit by the fireside
Munching bread and honey,

Watching them in mischief
From corners of their eyes,
Slily allowing them to lick
Honey-sticky fingers.

Sovereign against Lollocks
Are hard broom and soft broom,
To well comb the hair,
To well brush the shoe,
And to pay every debt
So soon as it's due.

Work in Hand March 1942

Despite and Still

Have you not read
The words in my head,
And I made part
Of your own heart?
We have been such as draw
The losing straw —
You of your gentleness,
I of my rashness,
Both of despair —
Yet still might share
This happy will:
To love despite and still.
Never let us deny
The thing's necessity,
But, O, refuse
To choose
Where chance may seem to give
Loves in alternative.

Work in Hand March 1942

Frightened Men

We are not of their kind, nor ever were,
Never having had such claws to our paws
In any hypothetic incarnation;
Have only the least knowledge of their minds
Through a grace on their part in thinking aloud;
And we remain mouse-quiet when they begin
Suddenly in their unpredictable way
To weave an allegory of their lives,
Making each point by walking round it –
Then off again, as interest is warmed.
What have they said? Or unsaid? What?
We understood the general drift only.

They are punctilious as implacable,
Most amiable with those who hate them most.
A shout will scare them. When they spring, they seize.
The worst is when they hide from us and change
To something altogether other:
We meet them at the door, as who returns
After a one-hour-seeming century
To a house not his own.

Work in Hand March 1942

The Oath

The doubt and the passion
Falling away from them,
    In that instant both
Take timely courage
From the sky's clearness
    To confirm an oath.

Her loves are his loves,
His trust is her trust;
    Else all were grief
And they, lost travellers
On a yellowing page,
    Death overleaf.

110

Rumour of old battle
Growls across the air;
    Then let it growl
With no more terror
Than the creaking stair
    Or the calling owl.

She knows, as he knows,
Of a faithful-always
    And an always-dear
By early emblems
Prognosticated,
    Fulfilled here.

Work in Hand March 1942

Language of the Seasons

Living among orchards, we are ruled
By the four seasons necessarily:
This from unseasonable frosts we learn
Or from usurping suns and haggard flowers –
Legitimist our disapproval.

Weather we knew, not seasons, in the city
While, seasonless, orange and orchid shone,
Knew it by heavy overcoat or light,
Framed love in later terminologies
Than here, where we report how weight of snow,
Or weight of fruit, tears branches from the tree.

Work in Hand March 1942

Mid-Winter Waking

Stirring suddenly from long hibernation
I knew myself once more a poet
Guarded by timeless principalities
Against the worm of death, this hillside haunting;
And presently dared open both my eyes.

O gracious, lofty, shone against from under,
Back-of-the-mind-far clouds like towers;
And you, sudden warm airs that blow
Before the expected season of new blossom,
While sheep still gnaw at roots and lambless go –

Be witness that on waking, this mid-winter,
I found her hand in mine laid closely
Who shall watch out the Spring with me.
We stared in silence all around us
But found no winter anywhere to see.

Work in Hand March 1942

Through Nightmare

Never be disenchanted of
That place you sometimes dream yourself into,
Lying at large remove beyond all dream,
Or those you find there, though but seldom
In their company seated –

The untameable, the live, the gentle.
Have you not known them? Whom? They carry
Time looped so river-wise about their house
There's no way in by history's road
To name or number them.

In your sleepy eyes I read the journey
Of which disjointedly you tell; which stirs
My loving admiration, that you should travel
Through nightmare to a lost and moated land,
Who are timorous by nature.

Wales January 1944

112

Instructions to the Orphic Adept

(In part translated from the Timpone Grande and Compagno Orphic tablets.

So soon as ever your mazed spirit descends
From daylight into darkness, Man, remember
What you have suffered here in Samothrace,
What you have suffered.

After your passage through Hell's seven floods,
Whose fumes of sulphur will have parched your throat,
The Halls of Judgement will loom up before you,
A miracle of jasper and of onyx.
To the left hand there bubbles a black spring
Overshadowed with a great white cypress.
Avoid this spring, which is Forgetfulness;
Though all the common rout rush down to drink,
Avoid this spring.

To the right hand there lies a secret pool
Alive with speckled trout and fish of gold;
A hazel overshadows it; Ophion,
Primaeval serpent straggling in the branches,
Darts out his tongue. This holy pool is fed
By dripping water; guardians stand before it.
Run to this pool, the pool of Memory,
Run to this pool.

Then will the guardians scrutinize you, saying:
'Who are you, who? What have you to remember?
Do you not fear Ophion's flickering tongue?
Go rather to the spring beneath the cypress,
Flee from this pool.'

Then you shall answer: 'I am parched with thirst.
Give me to drink. I am a child of Earth,
But of Sky also, come from Samothrace.
Witness the glint of amber on my brow.
Out of the Pure I come, as you may see.
I also am of your thrice-blessed kin,
Child of the three-fold Queen of Samothrace:
Have made full quittance for my deeds of blood,
Have been by her invested in sea-purple,
And like a kid have fallen into milk,
Give me to drink, now I am parched with thirst,
Give me to drink!'

113

But they will ask you yet: 'What of your feet?'
You shall reply: 'My feet have borne me here
Out of the weary wheel, the circling years,
To that still, spokeless wheel: – Persephone.
Give me to drink!'

Then they will welcome you with fruit and flowers,
And lead you toward the ancient dripping hazel,
Crying: 'Brother of our immortal blood,
Drink and remember glorious Samothrace!'
Then you shall drink.

You shall drink deep of that refreshing draught,
To become lords of the uninitiated
Twittering ghosts, Hell's countless populace –
To become heroes, knights upon swift horses,
Pronouncing oracles from your tall white tombs,
By the nymphs tended. They with honey water
Shall pour libations to your serpent shapes,
That you may drink.

Poems 1938-1945 November 1945

Theseus and Ariadne

High on his figured couch beyond the waves
He dreams, in dream recalling her set walk
Down paths of oyster-shell bordered with flowers
And down the shadowy turf beneath the vine.
He sighs: 'Deep sunk in my erroneous past
She haunts the ruins and the ravaged lawns.'

Yet still unharmed it stands, the regal house
Crooked with age and overtopped by pines
Where first he wearied of her constancy.
And with a surer foot she goes than when
Dread of his hate was thunder in the air,
When the pines agonized with flaws of wind
And flowers glared up at her with frantic eyes.

114

Of him, now all is done, she never dreams
But calls a living blessing down upon
What he would have mere rubble and rank grass;
Playing the queen to nobler company.

Poems 1938-1945 November 1945

To Juan at the Winter Solstice

There is one story and one story only
That will prove worth your telling,
Whether as learned bard or gifted child;
To it all lines or lesser gauds belong
That startle with their shining
Such common stories as they stray into.

Is it of trees you tell, their months and virtues,
Of strange beasts that beset you,
Of birds that croak at you the Triple will?
Or of the Zodiac and how slow it turns
Below the Boreal Crown,
Prison of all true kings that ever reigned?

Water to water, ark again to ark,
From woman back to woman:
So each new victim treads unfalteringly
The never altered circuit of his fate,
Bringing twelve peers as witness
Both to his starry rise and starry fall.

Or is it of the Virgin's silver beauty,
All fish below the thighs?
She in her left hand bears a leafy quince;
When with her right she crooks a finger, smiling,
How may the King hold back?
Royally then he barters life for love.

Or of the undying snake from chaos hatched,
Whose coils contain the ocean,
Into whose chops with naked sword he springs,

115

Then in black water, tangled by the reeds,
Battles three days and nights,
To be spewed up beside her scalloped shore?

Much snow is falling, winds roar hollowly,
The owl hoots from the elder,
Fear in your heart cries to the loving-cup:
Sorrow to sorrow as the sparks fly upward.
The log groans and confesses
There is one story and one story only.

Dwell on her graciousness, dwell on her smiling,
Do not forget what flowers
The great boar trampled down in ivy time.
Her brow was creamy as the long ninth wave,
Her sea-blue eyes were wild
But nothing promised that is not performed.

Poems 1938-1945 November 1945

To Be Named a Bear
('To Be Called a Bear')

Bears gash the forest trees
       To mark the bounds
Of their own hunting grounds;
They follow the wild bees
       Point by point home
       For love of honeycomb;
They browse on blueberries.

       Then should I stare
       If I am named a bear,
       And is it not the truth?
Unkempt and surly with a sweet tooth
I tilt my muzzle toward the starry hub
Where Queen Callisto guards her cub.

But envy those that here
    All winter breathing slow
    Sleep warm under the snow,
That yawn awake when the skies clear,
    And lank with longing grow
No more than one brief month a year.

Tomorrow October 1947

The Last Day of Leave (1916)

We five looked out over the moor
At rough hills blurred with haze, and a still sea:
Our tragic day, bountiful from the first.

We would spend it by the lily lake
(High in a fold beyond the farthest ridge),
Following the cart-track till it faded out.

The time of berries and bell-heather;
Yet all that morning nobody went by
But shepherds and one old man carting turfs.

We were in love: he with her, she with him,
And I, the youngest one, the odd man out,
As deep in love with a yet nameless muse.

No cloud; larks and heath-butterflies,
And herons undisturbed fishing the streams;
A slow cool breeze that hardly stirred the grass.

When we hurried down the rocky slope,
A flock of ewes galloping off in terror,
There shone the waterlilies, yellow and white.

Deep water and a shelving bank.
Off went our clothes and in we went, all five,
Diving like trout between the lily groves.

The basket had been nobly filled:
Wine and fresh rolls, chicken and pineapple –
Our braggadocio under threat of war.

The fire on which we boiled our kettle
We fed with ling and rotten blackthorn root;
And the coffee tasted memorably of peat.

Two of us might stray off together
But never less than three kept by the fire,
Focus of our uncertain destinies.

We spoke little, our minds in tune –
A sigh or laugh would settle any theme;
The sun so hot it made the rocks quiver.

But when it rolled down level with us,
Four pairs of eyes sought mine as if appealing
For a blind-fate-aversive afterword: –

'Do you remember the lily lake?
We were all there, all five of us in love,
No one yet killed, widowed or broken-hearted.'

Tomorrow November 1947

The Destroyer

Swordsman of the narrow lips,
Narrow hips and murderous mind
Fenced with chariots and ships,
By your joculators hailed
The mailed wonder of mankind,
Far to westward you have sailed.

You it was dared seize the throne
Of a blown and amorous prince
Destined to the Moon alone,
A lame, golden-heeled decoy,
Joy of hens that gape and wince
Inarticulately coy.

You who, capped with lunar gold
Like an old and savage dunce,
Let the central hearth go cold,
Grinned, and left us here your sword
Warden of sick fields that once
Sprouted of their own accord.

Gusts of laughter the Moon stir
That her Bassarids now bed
With the ignoble usurer
While an ignorant pale priest
Rides the beast with a man's head
To her long-omitted feast.

Collected Poems (1914-1947) April 1948

The Survivor

To die with a forlorn hope, but soon to be raised
By hags, the spoliers of the field; to elude their claws
And stand once more on a well-swept parade-ground,
Scarred and bemedalled, sword upright in fist
At head of a new undaunted company:

Is this joy? to be doubtless alive again,
And the others dead? Will your nostrils gladly savour
The fragrance, always new, of a first hedge-rose?
Will your ears be charmed by the thrush's melody
Sung as though he had himself devised it?

And is this joy: after the double suicide
(Heart against heart) to be restored entire,
To smooth your hair and wash away the life-blood,
And presently seek a young and innocent bride,
Whispering in the dark: 'for ever and ever'?

Tomorrow May 1951

Primrose and Periwinkle
('The Young Cordwainer')

SHE: Love, why have you led me here
      To this lampless hall,
A place of despair and fear
      Where blind things crawl?

HE: Not I, but your complaint
      Heard by the riverside
That primrose scent grew faint
      And desire died.

SHE: Kisses had lost virtue
      As you yourself must know;
I declared what, alas, was true
      And still shall do so.

HE: Mount, sweetheart, this main stair
      Where bandogs at the foot
Their crooked gilt teeth bare
      Between jaws of soot.

SHE: I loathe them, how they stand
      Like prick-eared spies.
Hold me fast by the left hand;
      I walk with closed eyes.

HE: Primrose has periwinkle
      As her mortal fellow:
Five leaves, blue and baleful,
      Five of true yellow.

SHE: Overhead, what's overhead?
      Where would you take me?
My feet stumble for dread,
      My wits forsake me.

HE: Flight on flight, floor above floor,
      In suspense of doom
To a locked secret door
      And a white-walled room.

SHE: Love, have you the pass-word,
   Or have you the key,
  With a sharp naked sword
   And wine to revive me?

HE: Enter: here is starlight,
   Here the state bed
  Where your man lies all night
   With blue flowers garlanded.

SHE: Ah, the cool open window
   Of this confessional!
  With wine at my elbow,
  And sword beneath the pillow,
   I shall perfect all.

New Statesman June 1951

The White Goddess

All saints revile her, and all sober men
Ruled by the God Apollo's golden mean –
In scorn of which we sailed to find her
In distant regions likeliest to hold her
Whom we desired above all things to know,
Sister of the mirage and echo.
It was a virtue not to stay,
To go our headstrong and heroic way
Seeking her out at the volcano's head,
Among pack ice, or where the track had faded
Beyond the cavern of the seven sleepers:
Whose broad high brow was white as any leper's,
Whose eyes were blue, with rowan-berry lips,
With hair curled honey-coloured to white hips.

The sap of Spring in the young wood a-stir
Will celebrate with green the Mother,
And every song-bird shout awhile for her;
But we are gifted, even in November

Rawest of seasons, with so huge a sense
Of her nakedly worn magnificence
We forget cruelty and past betrayal,
Heedless of where the next bright bolt may fall.

Poems and Satires November 1951

The Straw

Peace, the wild valley streaked with torrents,
A hoopoe perched on his warm rock. Then why
This tremor of the straw between my fingers?

What should I fear? Have I not testimony
In her own hand, signed with her own name
That my love fell as lightning on her heart?

These questions, bird, are not rhetorical.
Watch how the straw twitches and leaps
As though the earth quaked at a distance.

Requited love; but better unrequited
If this chance instrument gives warning
Of cataclysmic anguish far away.

Were she at ease, warmed by the thought of me,
Would not my hand stay steady as this rock?
Have I undone her by my vehemence?

Poetry December 1951

Rhea

On her shut lids the lightning flickers,
Thunder explodes above her bed,
An inch from her lax arm the rain hisses;
Discrete she lies,

Not dead but entranced, dreamlessly
With slow breathing, her lips curved
In a half-smile archaic, her breast bare,
Hair astream.

The house rocks, a flood suddenly rising
Bears away bridges: oak and ash
Are shivered to the roots – royal green timber.
She nothing cares.

(Divine Augustus, trembling at the storm,
Wrapped sealskin on his thumb; divine Caius
Made haste to hide himself in a deep cellar,
Distraught by fear.)

Rain, thunder, lightning: pretty children.
'Let them play,' her mother-mind repeats;
'They do no harm, unless from high spirits
Or by mishap.'

New Statesman July 1952

Esau and Judith

Robbed of his birthright and his blessing
Esau sought refuge in the wilderness,
An outlaw girding at the world's deceit.
He took to wife Judith, daughter of Heth,
Tall and grey-eyed, a priestess of her grove.
The curse lay heavy on their marriage-couch.

She was that sea which God had held corrupt;
Her tides he praised and her curvetting fish,
Though with no comprehension of their ways;
As a man blind from birth fondly adores
Fantasies of imagined gold and blue –
The curse lay heavy on their marriage-couch.

For how might Esau strive against his blood?
Had Isaac and Rebekah not commanded:
'Take thee a daughter from thy father's house!' —
Isaac who played the pander with Rebekah,
Even as Abraham had done with Sarah?
The curse lay heavy on their marriage-couch.

Poems 1953 September 1953

The Portrait

She speaks always in her own voice
Even to strangers; but those other women
Exercise their borrowed, or false, voices
Even on sons and daughters.

She can walk invisibly at noon
Along the high road; but those other women
Gleam phosphorescent — broad hips and gross fingers —
Down every lampless alley.

She is wild and innocent, pledged to love
Through all disaster; but those other women
Decry her for a witch or a common drab
And glare back when she greets them.

Here is her portrait, gazing sidelong at me,
The hair in disarray, the young eyes pleading:
'And you, love? As unlike those other men
As I those other women?'

Hudson Review Winter 1953

The Window Sill

Presage and caveat not only seem
To come in dream,
But do so come in dream.

When the cock crew and phantoms floated by,
This dreamer I
Out of the house went I,

Down long unsteady streets to a mad square;
And who was there,
Or whom did I know there?

Julia, leaning on her window sill.
'I love you still,'
Said she, 'O love me still!'

I answered: 'Julia, do you love me best?'
'What of this breast,'
She mourned, 'this flowery breast?'

Then a wild sobbing spread from door to door,
And every floor
Cried shame on every floor,

As she unlaced her bosom to disclose
Each breast a rose,
A white and cankered rose.

New Statesman October 1954

Counting the Beats

You, love, and I,
(He whispers) you and I,
And if no more than only you and I
What care you or I?

Counting the beats,
Counting the slow heart beats,
The bleeding to death of time in slow heart beats,
Wakeful they lie.

125

Cloudless day,
Night, and a cloudless day;
Yet the huge storm will burst upon their heads one day
From a bitter sky.

Where shall we be,
(She whispers) where shall we be,
When death strikes home, O where then shall we be
Who were you and I?

Not there but here,
(He whispers) only here,
As we are, here, together, now and here,
Always you and I.

Counting the beats,
Counting the slow heart beats,
The bleeding to death of time in slow heart beats,
Wakeful they lie.

Collected Poems 1955 June 1955

Darien

It is a poet's privilege and fate
To fall enamoured of the one Muse
Who variously haunts this island earth.

She was your mother, Darien,
And presaged by the darting halcyon bird
Would run green-sleeved along her ridges,
Treading the asphodels and heather-trees
With white feet bare.

Often at moonrise I had watched her go
And a cold shudder shook me
To see the curved blade of her Cretan axe.
Averted her set face, her business
Not yet with me, long-striding,
She would ascend the peak and pass from sight.
But once at full moon, by the sea's verge,
I came upon her without warning.

Unrayed she stood, with long hair streaming,
A cockle-shell cupped in her warm hands,
Her axe propped idly on a stone.
No awe possessed me, only a great grief;
Wanly she smiled, but would not lift her eyes
(As a young girl will greet the stranger).
I stood upright, a head taller than she.
'See who has come,' said I.

She answered: 'If I lift my eyes to yours
And our eyes marry, man, what then?
Will they engender my son Darien?
Swifter than wind, with straight and nut-brown hair,
Tall, slender-shanked, grey-eyed untameable;
Never was born, nor ever will be born
A child to equal my son Darien,
Guardian of the hid treasures of your world.'

I knew then by the trembling of her hands
For whom that flawless blade would sweep:
My own oracular head, swung by its hair.

'Mistress,' I cried, 'the times are evil
And you have charged me with their remedy.
O, where my head is now, let nothing be
But a clay counterfeit with nacre blink:
Only look up, so Darien may be born.

'He is the northern star, the spell of knowledge,
Pride of all hunters and all fishermen,
Your deathless fawn, an eaglet of your eyrie,
The topmost branch of your unfellable tree,
A tear streaking the summer night,
The new green of my hope.' Lifting her eyes,
She held mine for a lost eternity.
'Sweetheart,' said I, 'strike now, for Darien's sake!'

Collected Poems 1955 June 1955

A Slice of Wedding Cake

Why have such scores of lovely, gifted girls
   Married impossible men?
Simple self-sacrifice may be ruled out,
   And missionary endeavour, nine times out of ten.

Repeat 'impossible men': not merely rustic,
   Foul-tempered or depraved
(Dramatic foils chosen to show the world
   How well women behave, and always have behaved).

Impossible men: idle, illiterate,
   Self-pitying, dirty, sly,
For whose appearance even in City parks
   Excuses must be made to casual passers-by.

Has God's supply of tolerable husbands
   Fallen, in fact, so low?
Or do I always over-value woman
   At the expense of man?
                 Do I?
                    It might be so.

Steps November 1958

128

The Black Goddess (1960-1972)

From Graves's *Mammon and the Black Goddess* (1965), we learn that the White God-dess's successor is far less demanding of her servants and less cruel to her faithful lover. Indeed, Graves seems to suggest that she is the reward for loyal devotion to her sister Muse. The Black Goddess enriches the poet's sensual intuition and also introduces him to wisdom. In this new state of awareness, Graves finds fresh poetic inspiration and new metaphors with which to describe the nature of his experience, as in 'The Fetter' and 'Nothing Now Astonishes'. The poem 'The Black Goddess' shows the poet induced into a transcendental state in which he senses the mysteries of abiding love.

Graves's output in this period – nearly 450 poems – is a tribute both to his stamina and to the effectiveness of his new muse. Most of the poems are inspired by young women in whom Graves found the spirit of the Goddess incarnated. No longer paying homage to a cruel, distant deity, he celebrates real, sensuous women. His relationships with the four young muses, however, were not always as serene as the Black Goddess had promised, so Graves continued to chronicle love's set-backs and betrayals. But constancy does not go unrewarded, and the whispers between the muse-goddess and her servant are often pregnant with the excitement and creative energy that new love arouses.

Even the most ardent septuagenarians grow weary, however, and in the final poems of this section, Graves moves to examine his own immortality and the mystery of the art which he had practised so faithfully.

MAJOR POETRY VOLUMES:

More Poems 1961	London: Cassell, 1961
New Poems 1962	London: Cassell, 1962
Man Does, Woman Is	London: Cassell, 1964
Collected Poems 1965	London: Cassell, 1965
Poems 1965-1968	London: Cassell, 1968
Poems about Love	London: Cassell, 1969
Collected Poems 1975	London: Cassell, 1975

Under the Olives

We never would have loved had love not struck
Swifter than reason, and despite reason:
Under the olives, our hands interlocked,
We both fell silent:
Each listened for the other's answering
Sigh of unreasonableness –
Innocent, gentle, bold, enduring, proud.

Observer January 1961

Turn of the Moon

Never forget who brings the rain
In swarthy goatskin bags from a far sea:
It is the Moon as she turns, repairing
Damages of long drought and sunstroke.

Never count upon the rain, never foretell it,
For no power can bring rain
Except the Moon as she turns; and who can rule her?
She is prone to delay the necessary floods,
Lest such a gift might become obligation,
A month, or two, or three; then suddenly
Not relenting but by way of whim
Will perhaps conjure from the cloudless west
A single rain-drop to surprise with hope
Each haggard, upturned face.

Were the Moon a Sun, we would count upon her
To bring rain seasonably as she turned;
Yet no one thinks to thank the regular Sun
For shining fierce in summer, mild in winter –
Why should the Moon so drudge?

But if one night she brings us, as she turns,
Soft, steady, even, copious rain
That harms no leaf nor flower, but gently falls
Hour after hour, sinking to the tap roots,
And the sodden earth exhales at dawn
A long sigh scented with pure gratitude,
Such rain – the first rain of our lives, it seems,
Neither foretold, cajoled, nor counted on –
Is woman giving as she loves.

Observer January 1961

The Visitation

Drowsing in my chair of disbelief
I watch the door as it slowly opens –
A trick of the night wind?

Your slender body seems a shaft of moonlight
Against the door as it gently closes.
Do you cast no shadow?

Your whisper is too soft for credence,
Your tread like blossom drifting from a bough,
Your touch even softer.

You wear that sorrowful and tender mask
Which on high mountain tops in heather-flow
Entrances lonely shepherds;

And though a single word scatters all doubts
I quake for wonder at your choice of me:
Why, why and why?

Poems Selected By Himself 1961

The Winged Heart

Trying to read the news, after your visit,
When the words made little sense, I let them go;
And found my heart suddenly sprouting feathers.

Alone in the house, and the full honest rain
After a devil's own four-day sirocco
Still driving down in sheets across the valley –

How it hissed, how the leaves of the olives shook!
We had suffered drought since earliest April;
Here we were already in October.

I have nothing more to tell you. What has been said
Can never possibly be retracted now
Without denial of the large universe.

131

Some curse had fallen between us, a dead hand,
An inhalation of evil sucking up virtue:
Which left us no recourse, unless we turned

Improvident as at our first encounter,
Deriding practical care of how or where:
Your certitude must be my certitude.

And the tranquil blaze of sky etherializing
The circle of rocks and our own rain-wet faces,
Was that not worth a lifetime of pure grief?

New Poems 1962 October 1962

A Restless Ghost

Alas for obstinate doubt: the dread
Of error in supposing my heart freed,
All care for her stone dead!
Ineffably will shine the hills and radiant coast
Of early morning when she is gone indeed,
Her divine elements disbanded, disembodied
And through the misty orchards in love spread –
When she is gone indeed –
But still among them moves her restless ghost.

New Poems 1962 October 1962

The Septuagenarian

Youth is the ruggedest burden that can score
Your septuagenarian shoulder:
If you should threaten, as before, to powder
Rocks with bare heels, or rend the oak asunder
With naked fingers, you can now no more
Plead youthful benefit of metaphor.
Such unsubstantiated boasts will be
Substantial evidence of senility.

New Statesman April 1963

132

A Time of Waiting

The moment comes when my sound senses
Warn me to keep the pot at a quiet simmer,
Conclude no rash decisions, enter into
No random friendships, check the runaway tongue
And fix my mind in a close caul of doubt –
Which is more difficult, maybe, than to face
Night-long assaults of lurking furies.

The pool lies almost empty; I watch it nursed
By a thin stream. Such idle intervals
Are from waning moon to the new – a moon always
Holds the cords of my heart. Then patience, hands;
Dabble your nerveless fingers in the shallows;
A time shall come when she has need of them.

Atlantic October 1963

To Beguile and Betray

To beguile and betray, though pardonable in women,
Slowly quenches the divine need-fire
By true love kindled in them. Have you not watched
The immanent Goddess fade from their brows
When they make private to her mysteries
Some whip-scarred rogue from the hulks, some painted clown
From the pantomime – and afterwards accuse you
Of jealous hankering for the mandalot
Rather than horror and sick foreboding
That she will never return to the same house?

Virginia Quarterly Review Autumn 1963

133

The Oleaster

Each night for seven nights beyond the gulf
A storm raged, out of hearing, and crooked flashes
Of lightning animated us. Before the day-break
Rain fell munificently for the earth's need...

No, here they never plant the sweet olive
As some do (bedding slips in a prepared trench),
But graft it on the club of Hercules
The savage, inexpugnable oleaster
Whose roots and bole bunching from limestone crannies
Sprout impudent shoots born only to be lopped
Spring after Spring. Theirs is a loveless berry...

By mid-day we walk out, with naked feet,
Through pools on the road, gazing at waterfalls
Or a line of surf, but mostly at the trees
Whose elegant branches rain has duly blackened
And pressed their crowns to a sparkling silver.

Innumerable, plump with promise of oil,
The olives hang grass-green, in thankfulness
For a bitter sap and bitter New Year snows
That cleansed their bark...
                    Forgive me, dearest love,
If nothing I can say be strange or new.
I am no child of the hot South like you,
Though in rock rooted like an oleaster.

Man Does, Woman Is April 1964

The Black Goddess

Silence, words into foolishness fading,
Silence prolonged, of thought so secret
We hush the sheep-bells and the loud cicada.

And your black agate eyes, wide open, mirror
The released firebird beating his way
Down a whirled avenue of blues and yellows.

134

Should I not weep? Profuse the berries of love,
The speckled fish, the filberts and white ivy
Which you, with a half-smile, bestow
On your delectable broad land of promise
For me, who never before went gay in plumes.

Man Does, Woman Is April 1964

Lamia in Love

Need of this man was her ignoble secret:
Desperate for love, yet loathing to deserve it,
She wept pure tears of sorrow when his eyes
Betrayed mistrust in her impeccable lies.

Man Does, Woman Is April 1964

Ambience

The nymph of the forest, only in whose honour
These birds perform, provides an ambience
But never leads the chorus: even at dawn
When we awake to whistle, flute and pipe,
Astonished they can so extemporize
Their own parts, as it were haphazard
Each in his own time, yet avoid discordance
Or domineering, however virtuose
Or long sustained each voluntary of love.
The rare silences, too, appear like sound
Rather than pause for breath or meditation...
Nor is the same piece ever given twice.

Love Respelt July 1965

Between Hyssop and Axe

To know our destiny is to know the horror
Of separation, dawn oppressed by night:
Is, between hyssop and axe, boldly to prove
That gifted, each, with singular need for freedom
And haunted, both, by spectres of reproach,
We may yet house together without succumbing
To the low fever of domesticity
Or to the lunatic spin of aimless flight.

Love Respelt July 1965

The Red Shower

Live sparks rain from the central anvil
   In a red shower. Let all beware
Who read the event as history, frowning at
   What they may find of madness there:
   Felicity endangering despair.

Love Respelt July 1965

The Fetter

Concerned, against our wish, with a sick world,
Self-neglectful, tuned to knock or summons,
We make amends for follies not our own.

We have taken love through a thousand deaths;
Should either try to slip our iron fetter,
It bites yet deeper into neck and arm.

As for that act of supererogation,
The kiss in which we secretly concur,
Let laughter mitigate its quiet excess.

136

Could we, only, be a simple, bickering pair
In the tied cottage of a small estate
With no tasks laid on us except to dig,
Hoe, fatten geese and scrape the quarter's rent,
How admirable our close interdependence;
Our insecurity how fortunate!

Love Respelt July 1965

Deliverance

Lying disembodied under the trees
(Their slender trunks converged above us
Like rays of a five-fold star) we heard
A sudden whinnying from the dark hill.

Our implacable demon, foaled by love,
Never knew rein or saddle; though he drank
From a stream winding by, his blue pastures
Ranged far out beyond the stellar mill.

He had seared us two so close together
That death itself might not disjoin us;
It was impossible you could love me less,
It was impossible I could love you more.

We were no calculating lovers
But gasped in awe at our deliverance
From a too familiar prison,
And vainly puzzled how it was that now
We should never need to build another,
As each, time after time, had done before.

Love Respelt July 1965

Nothing Now Astonishes

A month of vigilance draws to its close
With silence of snow and the Northern Lights
In longed-for wordlessness.

This rainbow spanning our two worlds
Becomes more than a bridge between them
They fade into geography.

Variegated with the seven colours
We twist them into skeins for hide and seek
In a lovers' labyrinth.

Can I be astonished at male trembling
Of sea-horizons as you lean towards them?
Nothing now astonishes.

You change, from a running drop of pure gold
On a silver salver, to the white doe
In nut-groves harbouring.

Let me be changed now to an eight-petalled
Scarlet anemone that will never strain
For the circling butterfly.

Rest, my loud heart: your too exultant flight
Had raised the wing-beat to a roar
Drowning seraphic whispers.

Love Respelt July 1965

Song: dew-drop and diamond

The difference between you and her
(Whom I to you did once prefer)
Is clear enough to settle:
She like a diamond shone, but you
Shine like an early drop of dew
Poised on a red rose-petal.

The dew-drop carries in its eye
Mountain and forest, sea and sky,
With every change of weather;
Contrariwise, a diamond splits
The prospect into idle bits
That none can piece together.

Poems 1965-1968 1968

The Olive Yard

Now by a sudden shift of eye
The hitherto exemplary world
Takes on immediate wildness
And birds, trees, winds, and very letters
Of our childhood's alphabet, alter
Into rainbowed mysteries.

Flesh is no longer, but power;
Numbers, no longer arithmetical,
Dance like lambs, fly like doves;
And silence falls at last, though silken branches
Gently heave in the near olive-yard
And vague cloud labours on.

Whose was the stroke of summer genius
Flung from a mountain fastness
Where the griffon-vulture soars
That let us read our shrouded future
As easily as a book of prayer
Spread open upon the knee?

Poems 1965-1968 1968

The Unpenned Poem

Should I wander with no frown, these idle days,
My dark hair trespassing on its pale brow –
If so, without companionship or praise,
Must I revisit marshes where frogs croak
Like me, mimicking penitential ways?

Are you still anchored to my slow, warm heart
After long years of drawing nightly nearer
And visiting our haunted room, timely
Ruffling its corners with love's hidden mop?
And still must we not part?

What is a poem if as yet unpenned
Though truthful and emancipated still
From what may never yet appear,
From the flowery riches of still silent song
From golden hours of a wakeful Spring?

Approach me, Rhyme; advise me, Reason!
The wind blows gently from the mountain top.
Let me display three penetrative wounds
White and smooth in this wrinkled skin of mine,
Still unacknowledged by the flesh beneath.

A poem may be trapped here suddenly,
Thrusting its adder's head among the leaves,
Without reason or rhyme, dumb –
Or if not dumb, then with a single voice
Robbed of its chorus.

Here looms November. When last did I approach
Paper with ink, pen, and the half truth?
Advise me, Reason!

Collected Poems 1975 1975

140

The Green Woods of Unrest

Let the weeks end as well they must
Not with clouds of scattered dust
But in pure certainty of sun –
And with gentle winds outrun
By the love that we contest
In these green woods of unrest.
You, love, are beauty's self indeed,
Never the harsh pride of need.

Collected Poems 1975 1975

Index of First Lines

144

Robert Graves